U.S. Department
of Transportation

Federal Aviation
Administration

M000023498

FAA-S-ACS-8

(With Change 1)

Instrument Rating – Airplane

Airman Certification Standards

June 2016

**Flight Standards Service
Washington, DC 20591**

Acknowledgments

The U.S. Department of Transportation, Federal Aviation Administration (FAA), Airman Testing Standards Branch, AFS-630, and P.O. Box 25082, Oklahoma City, OK 73125 developed this Airman Certification Standards (ACS) document with the assistance of the aviation community. The FAA gratefully acknowledges the valuable support from the many individuals and organizations who contributed their time and expertise to assist in this endeavor.

Availability

This ACS is available for download from www.faa.gov. Please send comments regarding this document to AFS630comments@faa.gov.

Material in FAA-S-ACS-8 will be effective June 2016. All previous editions of the Instrument Rating – Airplane, Helicopter, and Powered Lift Practical Test Standards (FAA-S-8081-4E) will be obsolete as of this date for Airplane applicants. Helicopter and Powered Lift applicants should continue to use the FAA-S-8081-4E.

Foreword

The Federal Aviation Administration (FAA) has published the Instrument Rating Airplane Airman Certification Standards (ACS) document to communicate the aeronautical knowledge, risk management, and flight proficiency standards for the instrument rating (IR) in the airplane category, single-engine land and sea; and multiengine land and sea classes. This ACS incorporates and supersedes the previous Instrument Rating Practical Test Standards for Airplane, FAA-S-8081-4.

The FAA views the ACS as the foundation of its transition to a more integrated and systematic approach to airman certification. The ACS is part of the safety management system (SMS) framework that the FAA uses to mitigate risks associated with airman certification training and testing. Specifically, the ACS, associated guidance, and test question components of the airman certification system are constructed around the four functional components of an SMS:

- Safety Policy that defines and describes aeronautical knowledge, flight proficiency, and risk management as integrated components of the airman certification system;

- Safety Risk Management processes through which internal and external stakeholders identify and evaluate regulatory changes, safety recommendations, and other factors that require modification of airman testing and training materials;

- Safety Assurance processes to ensure the prompt and appropriate incorporation of changes arising from new regulations and safety recommendations; and

- Safety Promotion in the form of ongoing engagement with both external stakeholders (e.g., the aviation training industry) and FAA policy divisions.

The FAA has developed this ACS and its associated guidance in collaboration with a diverse group of aviation training experts. The goal is to drive a systematic approach to all components of the airman certification system, including knowledge test question development and conduct of the practical test. The FAA acknowledges and appreciates the many hours that these aviation experts have contributed toward this goal. This level of collaboration, a hallmark of a robust safety culture, strengthens and enhances aviation safety at every level of the airman certification system.

John S. Duncan
Director, Flight Standards Service

Revision History

Document#	Description	Effective Date
FAA-S-8081-4E	Instrument Rating for Airplane, Practical Test Standards (with Changes 1-5)	January 2010
FAA-S-ACS-8	Instrument Rating Airplane Airman Certification Standards	June 15, 2016
Change 1	Instrument Rating Airplane Airman Certification Standards	June 15, 2016

Record of Changes

Change 1 – June 15, 2016

- Corrected grammar and punctuation errors and capitalization inconsistencies throughout the document.

- Updated Appendix 9: References to include items missing from the previous version and remove items not in use.

- Updated Appendix 10: Abbreviations and Acronyms to include items missing or incorrect in the previous version.

Table of Contents

This page intentionally left blank.

Introduction

Airman Certification Standards Concept

The goal of the airman certification process is to ensure the applicant possesses knowledge and skill consistent with the privileges of the certificate or rating being exercised, as well as the ability to manage the risks of flight in order to act as pilot in command.

In fulfilling its responsibilities for the airman certification process, the Federal Aviation Administration (FAA) Flight Standards Service (AFS) plans, develops, and maintains materials related to airman certification training and testing. These materials include several components. The FAA knowledge test measures mastery of the aeronautical knowledge areas listed in Title 14 of the Code of Federal Regulations (14 CFR) part 61. Other materials, such as handbooks in the FAA H-8083 series, provide guidance to applicants on aeronautical knowledge, risk management, and flight proficiency.

The FAA recognizes that safe operations in today's complex National Airspace System (NAS) require a more systematic integration of aeronautical knowledge, risk management, and flight proficiency standards than those prescribed in the PTS. The FAA further recognizes the need to more clearly calibrate knowledge, risk management, and skills to the level of the certificate or rating, and to align standards with guidance and test questions.

To accomplish these goals, the FAA drew upon the expertise of organizations and individuals across the aviation and training community to develop the Airman Certification Standards (ACS). The ACS integrates the elements of knowledge, risk management, and skill listed in 14 CFR part 61 for each airman certificate or rating. It thus forms a more comprehensive standard for what an applicant must know, consider, and do for the safe conduct and successful completion of each Task to be tested on either the knowledge exam or the practical test.

The ACS significantly improves the knowledge test part of the certification process by enabling the development of test questions, from FAA reference documents, that are meaningful and relevant to safe operation in the NAS. The ACS does not change the tolerances for any skill Task, and it is important for applicants, instructors, and evaluators to understand that the addition of knowledge and risk management elements is not intended to lengthen or expand the scope of the practical test. Rather, the integration of knowledge and risk management elements associated with each Task is intended to enable a more holistic approach to learning, training, and testing. During the ground portion of the practical test, for example, the ACS provides greater context and structure both for retesting items missed on the knowledge test and for sampling the applicant's mastery of knowledge and risk management elements associated with a given skill Task.

Through the ground and flight portion of the practical test, the FAA expects evaluators to assess the applicant's mastery of the topic in accordance with the level of learning most appropriate for the specified Task. The oral questioning will continue throughout the entire practical test. For some topics, the evaluator will ask the applicant to describe or explain. For other items, the evaluator will assess the applicant's understanding by providing a scenario that requires the applicant to appropriately apply and/or correlate knowledge, experience, and information to the circumstances of the given scenario. The flight portion of the practical test requires the applicant to demonstrate knowledge, risk management, flight proficiency, and operational skill in accordance with the ACS.

Note: *As used in the ACS, an evaluator is any person authorized to conduct airman testing (e.g., an FAA aviation safety inspector, designated pilot examiner, or other individual authorized to conduct a test for a certificate or rating.)*

Using the ACS

The ACS consists of **Areas of Operation** arranged in a logical sequence, beginning with Preflight Preparation and ending with Postflight Procedures. Each Area of Operation includes **Tasks** appropriate to that Area of Operation. Each Task begins with an **Objective** stating what the applicant should know, consider, and/or do. The ACS then lists the aeronautical knowledge, risk management, and skill elements relevant to the specific Task, along with the conditions and standards for acceptable performance. The ACS uses **Notes** to emphasize special considerations. The ACS uses the terms "will" and "must" to convey directive (mandatory) information. The term "may" denotes items that are recommended but not required. The **References** for each Task indicate the source material for Task elements. For example, in Tasks such as "Current and forecast weather for departure, arrival, and en route phases of flight" (IR.I.B.K1), the applicant must be prepared for questions on any weather product presented in the references for that Task.

The abbreviation(s) within parentheses immediately following a Task refer to the category and/or class aircraft appropriate to that Task. The meaning of each abbreviation is as follows.

ASEL: Airplane – Single-Engine Land
ASES: Airplane – Single-Engine Sea
AMEL: Airplane – Multiengine Land
AMES: Airplane – Multiengine Sea

Note: When administering a test based on this ACS, the Tasks appropriate to the class airplane (ASEL, ASES, AMEL, or AMES) used for the test must be included in the plan of action. The absence of a class indicates the Task is for all classes.

Each Task in the ACS is coded according to a scheme that includes four elements. For example:

IR.I.C.K1:
IR = Applicable ACS (Instrument Rating – Airplane)
I = Area of Operation (Preflight Preparation)
A = Task (Cross-Country Flight Planning)
K1 = Task Element Knowledge 1 (Fuel planning)

Knowledge test questions are mapped to the ACS codes, which will soon replace the system of "Learning Statement Codes." After this transition occurs, the airman knowledge test report will list an ACS code that correlates to a specific Task element for a given Area of Operation and Task. Remedial instruction and re-testing will be specific, targeted, and based on specified learning criteria. Similarly, a Notice of Disapproval for the practical test will use the ACS codes to identify the deficient Task element(s).

The current knowledge test management system does not have the capability to print ACS codes. Until a new test management system is in place, the Learning Statement Codes (e.g., "PLT" codes will continue to be displayed on the Airman Knowledge Test Report (AKTR). The PLT codes are linked to references leading to broad subject areas. By contrast, each ACS code is tied to a unique Task element in the ACS itself. Because of this fundamental difference, there is no one-to-one correlation between LSC (PLT) codes and ACS codes.

Because all active knowledge test questions for the instrument rating airplane (IRA) knowledge test have been aligned with the corresponding ACS, evaluators can use PLT codes in conjunction with the ACS for a more targeted retesting of missed knowledge. The evaluator should look up the PLT code(s) on the applicant's AKTR in the Learning Statement Reference Guide. After noting the subject area(s), the evaluator can use the corresponding Area(s) of Operation/Task(s) in the ACS to narrow the scope of material for retesting, and to evaluate the applicant's understanding of that material in the context of the appropriate ACS Area(s) of Operation and Task(s).

Applicants for a combined private pilot certificate with instrument rating, in accordance with 14 CFR part 61, section 61.65 (a) and (g), must pass all areas designated in the Private Pilot Airplane ACS and the Instrument Rating Airplane ACS. Examiners need not duplicate Tasks. For example, only one preflight demonstration would be required; however, the Preflight Task from the Instrument Rating Airplane ACS would be more extensive than the Preflight Task from the Private Pilot Airplane ACS to ensure readiness for Instrument Flight Rules (IFR) flight.

A combined checkride should be treated as one practical test, requiring only one application and resulting in only one temporary certificate, disapproval notice, or letter of discontinuance, as applicable. Failure of any Task will result in a failure of the entire test and application. Therefore, even if the deficient maneuver was instrument related and the performance of all visual flight rules (VFR) Tasks was determined to be satisfactory, the applicant will receive a notice of disapproval.

The applicant must pass the instrument rating airplane knowledge test before taking the instrument rating practical test. The practical test is conducted in accordance with the ACS that is current as of the date of the test. Further, the applicant must pass the ground portion of the practical test before beginning the flight portion. The ground portion of the practical test allows the evaluator to determine whether the applicant is sufficiently prepared to advance to the flight portion of the practical test. The oral questioning will continue throughout the entire practical test.

The FAA encourages applicants and instructors to use the ACS to measure progress during training, and as a reference to ensure the applicant is adequately prepared for the knowledge and practical tests. The FAA will revise the ACS as circumstances require.

I. Preflight Preparation

Task A. Pilot Qualifications

References	14 CFR part 61; FAA-H-8083-2, FAA-H-8083-15
Objective	To determine the applicant exhibits satisfactory knowledge, risk management, and skills associated with the requirements to act as Pilot-in-Command (PIC) under Instrument Flight Rules (IFR).
Knowledge	The applicant demonstrates understanding of:
IR.I.A.K1	1. When an instrument rating is required.
IR.I.A.K2	2. Recent instrument flight experience requirements.
IR.I.A.K3	3. When flights conducted under actual or simulated IMC can be logged for instrument currency.
IR.I.A.K4	4. Pilot logbook/record-keeping requirements.
IR.I.A.K5	5. Physiological factors that might affect the pilot's ability to fly under instrument conditions.
Risk Management	The applicant demonstrates the ability to identify, assess and mitigate risks, encompassing:
IR.I.A.R1	1. Distinguishing proficiency versus currency.
IR.I.A.R2	2. Setting personal minimums.
Skills	The applicant demonstrates the ability to:
IR.I.A.S1	1. Act as PIC under IFR in a scenario provided by the evaluator.

Task B. Weather Information

References	14 CFR parts 61, 91; FAA-H-8083-2, FAA-H-8083-15; AC 00-6; AC 00-45, AIM
Objective	To determine the applicant exhibits satisfactory knowledge, risk management, and skills associated with obtaining, understanding, and applying weather information for a flight under IFR.

Knowledge	The applicant demonstrates understanding of:
IR.I.B.K1	1. Current and forecast weather for departure, en route, and arrival.
IR.I.B.K2	2. Meteorology to include:
IR.I.B.K2a	a. Weather system formation, including air masses and fronts
IR.I.B.K2b	b. Cloud types and hazards
IR.I.B.K2c	c. Turbulence
IR.I.B.K2d	d. Thunderstorms and microbursts
IR.I.B.K2e	e. Fog
IR.I.B.K2f	f. Types and hazards of icing to include frost
IR.I.B.K2g	g. Atmosphere/temperature
IR.I.B.K2h	h. Wind (e.g., crosswind, tailwind, wind shear, etc.)
IR.I.B.K2i	i. Moisture/precipitation
IR.I.B.K3	3. En route weather resources.
Risk Management	The applicant demonstrates the ability to identify, assess and mitigate risks, encompassing:
IR.I.B.R1	1. The limitations of aviation weather reports and forecasts.
IR.I.B.R2	2. The limitations of inflight aviation weather resources.
IR.I.B.R3	3. Identification of alternate airports along the intended route of flight and circumstances that would make diversion prudent.
IR.I.B.R4	4. Hazardous weather conditions that may affect the planned flight.
IR.I.B.R5	5. Known or forecast icing conditions.
Skills	The applicant demonstrates the ability to:
IR.I.B.S1	1. Use available aviation weather resources to obtain an adequate weather briefing.
IR.I.B.S2	2. Correlate weather information to determine if an alternate is required and ensure the selected alternate airport meets regulatory requirements.
IR.I.B.S3	3. Correlate weather information to make a competent go/no-go decision.
IR.I.B.S4	4. Obtain weather during flight.

Task C. Cross-Country Flight Planning

References	14 CFR part 91; FAA-H-8083-2, FAA-H-8083-15, FAA-H-8083-16, FAA-H-8083-25; Chart Supplements U.S.; AIM
Objective	To determine the applicant exhibits satisfactory knowledge, risk management, and skills associated with planning an IFR cross-country and filing an IFR flight plan.

Knowledge	The applicant demonstrates understanding of:
IR.I.C.K1	1. Fuel planning.
IR.I.C.K2	2. Definitions of minimum or emergency fuel.
IR.I.C.K3	3. Conditions conducive to icing, wind shear, microbursts, and turbulence.
IR.I.C.K4	4. Symbology found on IFR en route and approach charts and diagrams.
IR.I.C.K5	5. Where to locate and how to apply preferred IFR routing.
IR.I.C.K6	6. Elements and operational requirements of an IFR flight plan.
IR.I.C.K7	7. Procedures for activating and closing an IFR flight plan in controlled and uncontrolled airspace.
IR.I.C.K8	8. Oxygen requirements.
IR.I.C.K9	9. Altitude and course requirements.
IR.I.C.K10	10. Preflight requirements.
IR.I.C.K11	11. Airspace, cloud clearance, and visibility requirements.
IR.I.C.K12	12. Alternate airport selection.
IR.I.C.K13	13. Adequate knowledge of Global Positioning System (GPS) and Receiver Autonomous Integrity Monitoring (RAIM) capability, when the aircraft is so equipped.

Risk Management	The applicant demonstrates the ability to identify, assess and mitigate risks, encompassing:
IR.I.C.R1	1. IFR altitude selection.
IR.I.C.R2	2. Dynamic weather.
IR.I.C.R3	3. Inadvertent icing encounters.
IR.I.C.R4	4. The limitations of ATC radar advisories.
IR.I.C.R5	5. Improper fuel planning.
IR.I.C.R6	6. Scenarios and circumstances associated with declaring minimum or emergency fuel.
IR.I.C.R7	7. A route involving significant environmental influences, mountains, or large bodies of water.
IR.I.C.R8	8. Human factors that may impact making an initial go/no-go decision and the decision to continue the flight based upon an ongoing evaluation of the flight.
IR.I.C.R9	9. Flight in areas unsuitable for landing or below personal weather minimums.

Skills	The applicant demonstrates the ability to:
IR.I.C.S1	1. Recalculate fuel reserves based on a scenario provided by the evaluator.
IR.I.C.S2	2. Explain, create and simulate filing an IFR flight plan for a route assigned by the evaluator, using actual weather reports/forecasts and conforming to the regulatory requirements for IFR within the airspace in which the flight will be conducted (preplanning is at evaluator's discretion).
IR.I.C.S3	3. Interpret departure, en route, arrival, and instrument approach procedures and charts.
IR.I.C.S4	4. Select a suitable alternate.
IR.I.C.S5	5. Calculate time en route and fuel considering factors such as power settings, operating altitude, wind, and fuel reserve requirements, and weight and balance requirements.
IR.I.C.S6	6. Obtain and correctly interprets applicable NOTAM information.
IR.I.C.S7	7. Determine the calculated performance is within the aircraft's capability and operating limitations.

II. Preflight Procedures

Task A. Aircraft Systems Related to IFR Operations

References	14 CFR parts 61, 91; FAA-H-8083-2, FAA-H-8083-15; AFM; AC 91-74
Objective	To determine the applicant exhibits satisfactory knowledge, risk management, and skills associated with anti-icing and de-icing systems.
Knowledge	The applicant demonstrates understanding of:
IR.II.A.K1	1. The general operational characteristics and limitations of anti-icing and deicing equipment.
Risk Management	The applicant demonstrates the ability to identify, assess and mitigate risks, encompassing:
IR.II.A.R1	1. Fuselage, wing, tail plane, propeller, carburetor and intake, fuel, and pitot-static icing.
IR.II.A.R2	2. Anti-icing and deicing equipment limitations.
IR.II.A.R3	3. Considerations of pilot and systems for flight into known or unforecast icing conditions.
Skills	The applicant demonstrates the ability to:
IR.II.A.S1	1. Simulate how to operate the anti-icing and deicing equipment applicable to their aircraft.

Task B. Aircraft Flight Instruments and Navigation Equipment

References	14 CFR parts 61, 91; FAA-H-8083-15
Objective	To determine the applicant exhibits satisfactory knowledge, risk management, and skills associated with managing instruments appropriate for an IFR flight.
Knowledge	The applicant demonstrates understanding of:
IR.II.B.K1	1. The general operation of flight instruments.
IR.II.B.K1a	a. Pitot-static system
IR.II.B.K1b	b. Gyroscopic/electric instruments
IR.II.B.K1c	c. Magnetic compass
IR.II.B.K1d	d. Transponder/altitude encoding
IR.II.B.K1e	e. Vacuum systems
IR.II.B.K2	2. The general characteristics of navigation instruments.
IR.II.B.K2a	a. NAVAIDs
IR.II.B.K2b	b. VOR
IR.II.B.K2c	c. DME
IR.II.B.K2d	d. RNAV
IR.II.B.K2e	e. ILS and marker beacon receiver/indications
IR.II.B.K2f	f. Flight Management System (FMS), GPS and RAIM capability
IR.II.B.K3	3. The general characteristics and common failure modes of autopilot systems.
IR.II.B.K4	4. Common failure modes of flight and navigation instruments.
IR.II.B.K5	5. The difference between approved and non-approved navigation devices.
IR.II.B.K6	6. The limitations of portable navigation devices for guidance or reference.
IR.II.B.K7	7. Electronic flight instrument displays (PFD, MFD).
Risk Management	The applicant demonstrates the ability to identify, assess and mitigate risks, encompassing:
IR.II.B.R1	1. Failure to manage the automation management.
IR.II.B.R2	2. The operation and interpretation of unfamiliar flight and navigation instruments.
IR.II.B.R3	3. Distractions created by programming advanced avionics.
IR.II.B.R4	4. The limitations of electronic flight bags.
Skills	The applicant demonstrates the ability to:
IR.II.B.S1	1. Operate and manage installed instruments and navigation equipment.

Task C. Instrument and Equipment Cockpit Check

References	14 CFR parts 61,91; FAA-H-8083-15
Objective	To determine the applicant exhibits satisfactory knowledge, risk management, and skills associated with conducting a preflight check on the aircraft instruments necessary for an IFR flight.
Knowledge	The applicant demonstrates understanding of:
IR.II.C.K1	1. The purpose of performing an instrument cockpit check and how to detect possible defects.
IR.II.C.K2	2. The procedures and required documentation for flying with inoperative equipment.
IR.II.C.K3	3. The limitations of flying with inoperative equipment.
IR.II.C.K4	4. The requirement for having a current aviation database.
IR.II.C.K5	5. The required equipment for IFR flight.
IR.II.C.K6	6. IFR airworthiness to include aircraft inspection requirements.
Risk Management	The applicant demonstrates the ability to identify, assess and mitigate risks, encompassing:
IR.II.C.R1	1. Inoperative equipment.
IR.II.C.R2	2. Programming avionics during aircraft movement.
IR.II.C.R3	3. Outdated navigation publications or databases.
Skills	The applicant demonstrates the ability to:
IR.II.C.S1	1. Perform an adequate preflight inspection of installed flight instruments, avionics, and navigation equipment by following the checklist appropriate to the aircraft and determine the aircraft is in condition for safe instrument flight.
IR.II.C.S2	2. Determine if the aircraft is legal and safe to fly in the event of inoperative equipment.
IR.II.C.S3	3. Properly document inoperative equipment as appropriate.
IR.II.C.S4	4. Determine if databases are current.
IR.II.C.S5	5. Aircraft movement preplanning to avoid runway incursions.

III. Air Traffic Control Clearances and Procedures

Task A. Compliance with Air Traffic Control Clearances

References	14 CFR parts 61, 91; FAA-H-8083-15; AIM
Objective	To determine the applicant exhibits satisfactory knowledge, risk management, and skills associated with ATC clearances and procedures. **Note:** *The ATC clearance may be an actual or simulated ATC clearance based upon the flight plan.*

Knowledge	The applicant demonstrates understanding of:
IR.III.A.K1	1. The responsibilities associated with accepting an ATC clearance.
IR.III.A.K2	2. The requirements to read back an ATC clearance.
IR.III.A.K3	3. Pilot in Command (PIC) emergency authority.
IR.III.A.K4	4. The methods to obtain an ATC clearance.
IR.III.A.K5	5. Terrain clearance requirements associated with departure procedures.
IR.III.A.K6	6. Lost communication procedures.
IR.III.A.K7	7. The purpose of "expect" in a clearance.
IR.III.A.K8	8. The procedures involved for the departure, en route, and arrival phases of flight.
IR.III.A.K9	9. Position reporting.
IR.III.A.K10	10. The purpose and use of clearance void times.

Risk Management	The applicant demonstrates the ability to identify, assess and mitigate risks, encompassing:
IR.III.A.R1	1. Failure to fully understand an ATC clearance.
IR.III.A.R2	2. Inappropriate, incomplete, or incorrect ATC clearances.
IR.III.A.R3	3. ATC clearances inconsistent with aircraft performance and /or navigation capability to comply.
IR.III.A.R4	4. Short clearance void times.
IR.III.A.R5	5. Airborne clearances.
IR.III.A.R6	6. Flying IFR in a non-radar environment.
IR.III.A.R7	7. Similar aircraft call signs and the risks of accepting another aircraft's ATC instruction.
IR.III.A.R8	8. The use of outdated navigation publications and databases.
IR.III.A.R9	9. Collision, obstacle, and terrain avoidance.

Skills	The applicant demonstrates the ability to:
IR.III.A.S1	1. Use and understand standard phraseology.
IR.III.A.S2	2. Correctly copy, read back, interpret, and comply with an ATC clearance.
IR.III.A.S3	3. Correctly set up communication frequencies, navigation systems and transponder codes in compliance with the ATC clearance.
IR.III.A.S4	4. Establish two-way communication with the proper controlling agency, in a timely manner, and use standard phraseology.
IR.III.A.S5	5. Maintain the applicable airspeed within ±10 knots; headings within ±10°, altitude within ±100 feet and tracks a course, radial, or bearing within ¾- scale deflection of the CDI on a procedure.

Task B. Holding Procedures

References	14 CFR parts 61, 91; FAA-H-8083-15; AIM
Objective	To determine the applicant exhibits satisfactory knowledge, risk management, and skills associated with holding procedures.
Knowledge	The applicant demonstrates understanding of:
IR.III.B.K1	1. The purpose of holding.
IR.III.B.K2	2. Reporting criteria associated with holding patterns.
IR.III.B.K3	3. Recommended entry procedures and holding speeds.
IR.III.B.K4	4. The reporting criteria associated with minimum and emergency fuel.
IR.III.B.K5	5. Applying wind corrections to the holding pattern.
IR.III.B.K6	6. Using the autopilot (if equipped) for holding.
Risk Management	The applicant demonstrates the ability to identify, assess and mitigate risks, encompassing:
IR.III.B.R1	1. Fuel reserves if assigned an unanticipated expect further clearance (EFC) time.
IR.III.B.R2	2. Scenarios and circumstances associated with declaring minimum or emergency fuel.
IR.III.B.R3	3. Scenarios that could lead to holding.
IR.III.B.R4	4. Deteriorating weather while in holding or at the destination.
IR.III.B.R5	5. Improper holding entry.
IR.III.B.R6	6. Improper wind correction while holding.
IR.III.B.R7	7. Failure to maintain the proper holding airspeed.
IR.III.B.R8	8. Improper management of the navigation system or automation while holding.
Skills	The applicant demonstrates the ability to:
IR.III.B.S1	1. Update fuel reserve calculations based on expect further clearance times.
IR.III.B.S2	2. Maintain the airspeed within ±10 knots; altitude within ±100 feet; headings within ±10°; and track a selected course, radial or bearing within ¾-scale deflection of the CDI.
IR.III.B.S3	3. Use appropriate navigation displays, as supplementary devices, to maintain prescribed ground track.
IR.III.B.S4	4. Use proper wind correction procedures to maintain the desired pattern and to arrive over the fix as close as possible to a specified time.
IR.III.B.S5	5. Comply with restrictions, if applicable, associated with the holding pattern.
IR.III.B.S6	6. Set appropriate power settings for fuel conservation.
IR.III.B.S7	7. Change to the holding airspeed appropriate for the altitude or aircraft when 3 minutes or less from, but prior to arriving at, the holding fix.
IR.III.B.S8	8. Explain and use an entry procedure that ensures the aircraft remains within the holding pattern airspace for a standard, nonstandard, published, or non-published holding pattern.
IR.III.B.S9	9. Recognize arrival at the holding fix and initiate a prompt entry into the holding pattern.
IR.III.B.S10	10. Comply with ATC reporting requirements.
IR.III.B.S11	11. Use the proper timing criteria, where applicable, as required by altitude or ATC instructions and comply with pattern leg lengths when a leg length is specified.

IV. Flight by Reference to Instruments

Task A. Instrument Flight

References	14 CFR part 61; FAA-H-8083-15
Objective	To determine the applicant exhibits satisfactory knowledge, risk management, and skills associated with performing basic instrument flight maneuvers.
Knowledge	The applicant demonstrates understanding of:
IR.IV.A.K1	1. The concepts of instrument flight references related to attitude instrument flying during straight-and-level, climbs, turns, and descents.
IR.IV.A.K1a	a. Pitch instruments
IR.IV.A.K1b	b. Bank instruments
IR.IV.A.K1c	c. Power instruments
IR.IV.A.K2	2. Spatial disorientation and optical illusions.
IR.IV.A.K3	3. Normal and abnormal instrument indications.
IR.IV.A.K4	4. Normal and abnormal instrument operations.
Risk Management	The applicant demonstrates the ability to identify, assess and mitigate risks, encompassing:
IR.IV.A.R1	1. Situations that can degrade a pilots instrument cross-check.
IR.IV.A.R2	2. Distractions created by passengers.
IR.IV.A.R3	3. Physiological factors that can degrade a pilots instrument cross-check.
IR.IV.A.R4	4. Failure to recognize an abnormal instrument indication.
IR.IV.A.R5	5. Flying with unfamiliar flight display systems.
Skills	The applicant demonstrates the ability to:
IR.IV.A.S1	1. Maintain altitude within ±100 feet during level flight, headings within ±10°, airspeed within ±10 knots, and bank angles within ±5° during turns.
IR.IV.A.S2	2. Use proper instrument cross-check and interpretation, and apply the appropriate pitch, bank, power, and trim corrections when applicable.

Task B. Recovery from Unusual Flight Attitudes

References	14 CFR part 61; FAA-H-8083-15
Objective	To determine the applicant exhibits satisfactory knowledge, risk management, and skills associated with recovering from unusual flight attitudes.
Knowledge	The applicant demonstrates understanding of:
IR.IV.B.K1	1. Physiological factors that can lead to, or hinder recovery from an unusual attitude.
IR.IV.B.K2	2. Systems and equipment failures that could lead to an unusual attitude.
IR.IV.B.K3	3. Environmental factors that can lead to an unusual attitude.
IR.IV.B.K4	4. The recovery procedures to restore the aircraft to a normal flight attitude.
Risk Management	The applicant demonstrates the ability to identify, assess and mitigate risks, encompassing:
IR.IV.B.R1	1. Situations that could lead to loss of control.
IR.IV.B.R2	2. Unusual flight attitudes which can result from stress, high workload, task saturation, and distractions.
IR.IV.B.R3	3. Startle response during unexpected events.
IR.IV.B.R4	4. Failure to recognize an unusual flight attitude.
IR.IV.B.R5	5. Failure to follow the proper recovery procedures.
IR.IV.B.R6	6. Exceeding an operating limitation or operating outside of the normal flight envelope.
Skills	The applicant demonstrates the ability to:
IR.IV.B.S1	1. Recognize, confirm, and recover from unusual attitudes (nose-high and nose-low; low or high speed).
IR.IV.B.S2	2. Apply proper instrument cross-check and interpretation, and apply the appropriate pitch, bank, and power corrections, in the correct sequence, to return the aircraft to a stabilized level flight attitude.

V. Navigation Systems

Task A. Intercepting and Tracking Navigational Systems and DME Arcs

References	14 CFR parts 61, 91; FAA-H-8083-15; AFM; AIM
Objective	To determine the applicant exhibits satisfactory knowledge, risk management, and skills associated with intercepting and tracking navigation aids and DME arcs.
	Note: *The evaluator may disregard reference to specific navigational equipment if the aircraft is not equipped with those systems.*
Knowledge	The applicant demonstrates understanding of:
IR.V.A.K1	1. The procedures for intercepting and tracking courses and DME arcs.
IR.V.A.K2	2. Course guidance indications to include Horizontal Situation Indicator (HSI).
IR.V.A.K3	3. The indications of navigation systems failures.
Risk Management	The applicant demonstrates the ability to identify, assess and mitigate risks, encompassing:
IR.V.A.R1	1. Failure to perform proper course intercepts and tracking.
IR.V.A.R2	2. The use of secondary display information to intercept and track courses.
IR.V.A.R3	3. A navigation system failure.
IR.V.A.R4	4. Failure to manage the navigation automation.
Skills	The applicant demonstrates the ability to:
IR.V.A.S1	1. Tune and correctly identify the navigation facility.
IR.V.A.S2	2. Set and correctly orient to the course to be intercepted.
IR.V.A.S3	3. Intercept the specified course at a predetermined angle, inbound to or outbound from a navigational facility or waypoint
IR.V.A.S4	4. Maintain airspeed within ±10 knots, altitude within ±100 feet, and selected headings within ±5°.
IR.V.A.S5	5. Apply proper correction to maintain a course, allowing no more than ¾-scale deflection of the CDI.
IR.V.A.S6	6. Determine the aircraft position relative to the navigational facility or waypoint.
IR.V.A.S7	7. Intercept an arc and maintain that arc within ±1 nautical mile.
IR.V.A.S8	8. Recognize a navigational receiver or facility failure, and when required, report the failure to ATC.
IR.V.A.S9	9. Use a MFD and other graphical navigation displays, if installed, to monitor position, track wind drift, and other parameters to intercept and maintain the desired flight path.
IR.V.A.S10	10. Properly program the autopilot, if installed, to intercept courses.

Task B. Departure, En route and Arrival Operations

References	14 CFR parts 61, 91, FAA-H-8083-15; AC 91-74; AFM; AIM, AIM Pilot/Controller Glossary
Objective	To determine the applicant exhibits satisfactory knowledge, risk management, and skills associated with IFR departure, en route, and arrival operations.
Knowledge	The applicant demonstrates understanding of:
IR.V.B.K1	1. Departure Procedures (DPs).
IR.V.B.K2	2. ATC services available to pilots.
IR.V.B.K3	3. Pilot/Controller roles and responsibilities.
IR.V.B.K4	4. Instrument altitudes.
IR.V.B.K5	5. Airport lighting, signs, and markings.
IR.V.B.K6	6. Standard Terminal Arrival (STAR) procedures.
IR.V.B.K7	7. Communication during departure, en route, and arrival.
IR.V.B.K8	8. Instrument approach terms and abbreviations.
IR.V.B.K9	9. Instrument approach procedures (IAPs).
Risk Management	The applicant demonstrates the ability to identify, assess and mitigate risks, encompassing:
IR.V.B.R1	1. Icing conditions:
IR.V.B.R1a	a. Airframe
IR.V.B.R1b	b. Avoidance
IR.V.B.R1c	c. Exit strategy
IR.V.B.R1d	d. Static system
IR.V.B.R1e	e. Aerodynamics effects of airframe ice accumulation on performance and aircraft stability
IR.V.B.R2	2. Failure to use see and avoid techniques when appropriate.
IR.V.B.R3	3. Failure to recognize traffic avoidance equipment uses and limitations.
IR.V.B.R4	4. Failure to use the appropriate charts and database(s).
IR.V.B.R5	5. Terrain along the diversion flight path.
IR.V.B.R6	6. Failure to communicate with ATC or follow published procedures.
Skills	The applicant demonstrates the ability to:
IR.V.B.S1	1. Recognize changes to CDI scales/sensitivity.
IR.V.B.S2	2. Monitor ATC and use proper response(s).
IR.V.B.S3	3. Comply with published IAPs, DPs and STARs including any chart notes.
IR.V.B.S4	4. Use a VFR-on-Top clearance when issued.
IR.V.B.S5	5. Maintain an appropriate heading, climb and descent.
IR.V.B.S6	6. Use navigation systems/facilities for assistance, as appropriate for IFR flight.
IR.V.B.S7	7. Maintain airspeed within ±10 knots, altitude within ±100 feet, and selected headings within ±5°.
IR.V.B.S8	8. Apply proper correction to maintain a course, allowing no more than ¾-scale deflection of the CDI.

VI. Instrument Approach Procedures

Task A. Nonprecision Approach

References	14 CFR parts 61, 91; FAA-H-8083-15, FAA-H-8083-16; IAP, AIM
Objective	To determine the applicant exhibits satisfactory knowledge, risk management, and skills associated with performing nonprecision approach procedures.
	(see Appendix 7 – Aircraft, Equipment, and Operational Requirements & Limitations for related considerations)

Knowledge	The applicant demonstrates understanding of:
IR.VI.A.K1	1. Procedures and limitations associated with a nonprecision approach.
IR.VI.A.K2	2. The differences between Localizer Performance (LP) and Lateral Navigation (LNAV) approach guidance.
IR.VI.A.K3	3. Navigation system annunciations expected during a GPS based approach.

Risk Management	The applicant demonstrates the ability to identify, assess and mitigate risks, encompassing:
IR.VI.A.R1	1. Failure to follow prescribed procedures.
IR.VI.A.R2	2. Excessive descent rates.
IR.VI.A.R3	3. Deteriorating weather conditions on approach.
IR.VI.A.R4	4. An unstable approach.
IR.VI.A.R5	5. Failure to ensure proper aircraft configuration during an approach and missed approach.
IR.VI.A.R6	6. Descending below the minimum descent altitude (MDA) without proper visual references.
IR.VI.A.R7	7. Failure to manage the aircraft automation.

Skills	The applicant demonstrates the ability to:
IR.VI.A.S1	1. Select and comply with the appropriate instrument approach procedure to be performed.
IR.VI.A.S2	2. Establish two-way communications with ATC, as appropriate, to the phase of flight or approach segment, and uses proper communication phraseology.
IR.VI.A.S3	3. Select, tune, identify, and confirm the operational status of navigation equipment to be used for the approach procedure.
IR.VI.A.S4	4. Comply with all clearances issued by ATC or the evaluator.
IR.VI.A.S5	5. Recognize if any flight instrumentation is inaccurate or inoperative, and take appropriate action.
IR.VI.A.S6	6. Advise ATC or the evaluator anytime the aircraft is unable to comply with a clearance.
IR.VI.A.S7	7. Establish the appropriate aircraft configuration and airspeed considering turbulence and wind shear, and complete the aircraft checklist items appropriate to the phase of the flight.
IR.VI.A.S8	8. Maintain, prior to beginning the final approach segment, altitude within ±100 feet, heading within ±10° and allows less than ¾-scale deflection of the CDI, and maintain airspeed within ±10 knots.
IR.VI.A.S9	9. Apply the necessary adjustments to the published MDA and visibility criteria for the aircraft approach category when required such as:
IR.VI.A.S9a	a. Notices to Airmen (NOTAMs)
IR.VI.A.S9b	b. Inoperative aircraft and ground navigation equipment
IR.VI.A.S9c	c. Inoperative visual aids associated with the landing environment
IR.VI.A.S9d	d. National Weather Service reporting factors and criteria

(continued...)

(...continued)

Task A. Nonprecision Approach

IR.VI.A.S10	10. Establish a stabilized approach profile with a rate of descent and track that will ensure arrival at the MDA prior to reaching the missed approach point (MAP).
IR.VI.A.S11	11. Maintain, while on the final approach segment, no more than a ¾-scale deflection of the CDI, and maintain airspeed within ±10 knots of desired value.
IR.VI.A.S12	12. Maintain the MDA, when reached, within +100 feet, −0 feet to the MAP.
IR.VI.A.S13	13. Execute the missed approach procedure when the required visual references for the intended runway are not distinctly visible and identifiable at the MAP.
IR.VI.A.S14	14. Execute a normal landing from a straight-in or circling approach.
IR.VI.A.S15	15. Use a MFD and other graphical navigation displays, if installed, to monitor position, track wind drift and other parameters to maintain desired flight path.
IR.VI.A.S16	16. Confirm appropriate annunciations during a GPS-based approach.

Task B. Precision Approach

References	14 CFR parts 61, 91; FAA-H-8083-15, FAA-H-8083-16; IAP; AIM
Objective	To determine the applicant exhibits satisfactory knowledge, risk management, and skills associated with performing precision approach procedures. (see Appendix 7 – Aircraft, Equipment, and Operational Requirements & Limitations for related considerations)
Knowledge	The applicant demonstrates understanding of:
IR.VI.B.K1	1. The procedures and limitations associated with precision approach.
IR.VI.B.K2	2. The proper missed approach procedure associated with a FMS.
IR.VI.B.K3	3. The descent rates needed to follow the vertical guidance.
IR.VI.B.K4	4. How inoperative components can affect approach minimums.
Risk Management	The applicant demonstrates the ability to identify, assess and mitigate risks, encompassing:
IR.VI.B.R1	1. Failure to follow prescribed procedures.
IR.VI.B.R2	2. Descending below the decision altitude/decision height (DA/DH) without proper visual references.
IR.VI.B.R3	3. Failure to ensure proper aircraft configuration during an approach and missed approach.
IR.VI.B.R4	4. Deteriorating weather conditions on approach.
IR.VI.B.R5	5. An unstable approach.
IR.VI.B.R6	6. Failure to manage aircraft automation.
Skills	The applicant demonstrates the ability to:
IR.VI.B.S1	1. Establish two-way communications with ATC using the proper communications phraseology, as required for the phase of flight or approach segment.
IR.VI.B.S2	2. Comply, in a timely manner, with all clearances, instructions, and procedures.
IR.VI.B.S3	3. Advise ATC or the evaluator anytime the aircraft is unable to comply with a clearance.
IR.VI.B.S4	4. Establish the appropriate aircraft configuration and airspeed considering turbulence and wind shear, and complete the aircraft checklist items appropriate to the phase of the flight.
IR.VI.B.S5	5. Prior to beginning the final approach segment maintain the desired altitude±100 feet, the desired airspeed within ±10 knots, the desired heading within ±10°; and accurately track radials, courses, and bearings.
IR.VI.B.S6	6. Select tune, identify, and monitor the operational status of ground and airplane navigation equipment used for the approach.
IR.VI.B.S7	7. Apply the necessary adjustments to the published DA/DH and visibility criteria for the airplane approach category when required, such as:
IR.VI.B.S7a	a. NOTAMs
IR.VI.B.S7b	b. Inoperative airplane and ground navigation equipment
IR.VI.B.S7c	c. Inoperative visual aids associated with the landing environment
IR.VI.B.S7d	d. National Weather System reporting factors and criteria
IR.VI.B.S8	8. Establish a predetermined rate of descent at the point where the electronic glideslope begins, which approximates that required for the aircraft to follow the glideslope.
IR.VI.B.S9	9. Maintain a stabilized final approach, from the Final Approach Fix (FAF) to the DA/DH allowing no more than ¾- scale deflection of either the glideslope or localizer indications and maintain the desired airspeed within ±10 knots.

(continued...)

(...continued)

Task B. Precision Approach

IR.VI.B.S10	10. Initiate the missed approach procedures at the DA/DH, when the required visual references for the runway are not unmistakably visible and identifiable.
IR.VI.B.S11	11. Transition to a normal landing approach (missed approach for seaplanes) only when the aircraft is in a position from which a descent to a landing on the runway can be made at a normal rate of descent using normal maneuvering.
IR.VI.B.S12	12. Maintain the localizer and glideslope within ¾-scale deflection of the indicators during the visual descent from DA/DH to a point over the runway where the glideslope must be abandoned to accomplish a normal landing.
IR.VI.B.S13	13. Use a MFD and other graphical navigation displays, if installed, as appropriate to monitor position, track wind drift and other parameters to maintain the desired flight path.

Task C. Missed Approach

References	14 CFR parts 61, 91; FAA-H-8083-15; IAP; AIM
Objective	To determine the applicant exhibits satisfactory knowledge, risk management, and skills associated with performing a missed approach procedures.

Knowledge	The applicant demonstrates understanding of:
IR.VI.C.K1	1. The procedures and limitations associated with missed approach procedure.
IR.VI.C.K2	2. Missed approach procedures associated with a FMS, if equipped.
IR.VI.C.K3	3. Proper autopilot management procedures associated with missed approach procedure.

Risk Management	The applicant demonstrates the ability to identify, assess and mitigate risks, encompassing:
IR.VI.C.R1	1. Failure to follow prescribed procedures.
IR.VI.C.R2	2. Holding, diverting, or electing to fly the approach again.
IR.VI.C.R3	3. Failure to ensure proper aircraft configuration during an approach and missed approach.
IR.VI.C.R4	4. Executing a missed approach procedure before the MAP and the consequences.
IR.VI.C.R5	5. Failure to manage the aircraft automation.

Skills	The applicant demonstrates the ability to:
IR.VI.C.S1	1. Initiate the missed approach promptly by applying power, establishing a climb attitude, and reducing drag in accordance with the aircraft manufacturer's recommendations.
IR.VI.C.S2	2. Report to ATC upon beginning the missed approach procedure.
IR.VI.C.S3	3. Comply with the published or alternate missed approach procedure.
IR.VI.C.S4	4. Advise ATC or the evaluator anytime the aircraft is unable to comply with a clearance, restriction, or climb gradient.
IR.VI.C.S5	5. Follow the recommended checklist items appropriate to the missed approach/go-around procedure.
IR.VI.C.S6	6. Request, if appropriate, ATC clearance to the alternate airport, clearance limit, or as directed by the evaluator.
IR.VI.C.S7	7. Maintain the recommended airspeed within ±10 knots; heading, course, or bearing within ±10°; and altitude(s) within ±100 feet during the missed approach procedure.
IR.VI.C.S8	8. Use a MFD and other graphical navigation displays, if installed, to monitor position and track to help navigate the missed approach.

Task D. Circling Approach

References	14 CFR parts 61, 91; FAA-H-8083-15; IAP; AIM
Objective	To determine the applicant exhibits satisfactory knowledge, risk management, and skills associated with performing a circling approach procedure.

Knowledge	The applicant demonstrates understanding of:
IR.VI.D.K1	1. The procedures and limitations associated with a circling approach.
IR.VI.D.K2	2. Approach categories and relevant airspeed limitations.

Risk Management	The applicant demonstrates the ability to identify, assess and mitigate risks, encompassing:
IR.VI.D.R1	1. Failure to follow prescribed circling approach procedures.
IR.VI.D.R2	2. Executing a circling approach at night.
IR.VI.D.R3	3. Losing sight of the runway during a circling approach.
IR.VI.D.R4	4. Performing a circling approach in marginal visibility.
IR.VI.D.R5	5. Failure to manage the aircraft automation.
IR.VI.D.R6	6. Failure to maintain an appropriate airspeed while circling.
IR.VI.D.R7	7. Low altitude maneuvering.
IR.VI.D.R8	8. Executing a missed approach after the MAP while circling.

Skills	The applicant demonstrates the ability to:
IR.VI.D.S1	1. Select and comply with the circling approach procedure considering turbulence and wind shear and considering the maneuvering capabilities of the aircraft.
IR.VI.D.S2	2. Confirm the direction of traffic and adhere to all restrictions and instructions issued by ATC and the evaluator.
IR.VI.D.S3	3. Not circle beyond visibility requirement and maintain the appropriate circling altitude until in a position from which a descent to a normal landing can be made.
IR.VI.D.S4	4. Maneuver the aircraft after reaching the MDA on a flight path that will permit a normal landing on a runway. Maintain altitude +100 feet, -0 feet until a descent to a normal landing can be made. The runway selected must be such that it requires at least a 90° change of direction, from the final approach course, to align the aircraft for landing.

Task E. Landing from an Instrument Approach

References	14 CFR parts 61, 91; FAA-H-8083-15; AIM
Objective	To determine the applicant exhibits satisfactory knowledge, risk management, and skills associated with performing the procedures for a landing from an instrument approach.
Knowledge	The applicant demonstrates understanding of:
IR.VI.E.K1	1. The procedures and limitations associated with landing from an instrument approach.
IR.VI.E.K2	2. The purpose of a stabilized approach.
IR.VI.E.K3	3. Regulatory requirements for landing from an instrument approach.
IR.VI.E.K4	4. Approach lighting systems.
IR.VI.E.K5	5. Land and hold short operations (LAHSO) or option to refuse a LAHSO clearance.
IR.VI.E.K6	6. Airport signs, markings and lighting.
IR.VI.E.K7	7. Approach and landing hazards.
Risk Management	The applicant demonstrates the ability to identify, assess and mitigate risks, encompassing:
IR.VI.E.R1	1. Attempting to land from an unstable approach.
IR.VI.E.R2	2. Flying below the glidepath.
IR.VI.E.R3	3. Runway incursion after landing.
IR.VI.E.R4	4. The transition from instrument to visual references for landing.
Skills	The applicant demonstrates the ability to:
IR.VI.E.S1	1. Transition at the DA/DH, MDA, or visual descent point VDP to a visual flight condition, allowing for safe visual maneuvering and a normal landing.
IR.VI.E.S2	2. Adhere to all ATC (or evaluator) advisories, such as NOTAMs, wind shear, wake turbulence, runway surface, braking conditions, and other operational considerations.
IR.VI.E.S3	3. Complete the appropriate checklist items for the pre-landing and landing phase.
IR.VI.E.S4	4. Maintain positive aircraft control throughout the complete landing maneuver.

VII. Emergency Operations

Task A. Loss of Communications

References	14 CFR parts 61, 91; AIM
Objective	To determine the applicant exhibits satisfactory knowledge, risk management, and skills associated with loss of communications.
Knowledge	The applicant demonstrates understanding of:
IR.VII.A.K1	1. Procedures for lost communication during various phases of flight.
IR.VII.A.K2	2. The criteria for beginning an approach procedure at the destination with lost communications.
IR.VII.A.K3	3. When to deviate from an IFR clearance with lost communications.
IR.VII.A.K4	4. Techniques for re-establishing communications.
Risk Management	The applicant demonstrates the ability to identify, assess and mitigate risks, encompassing:
IR.VII.A.R1	1. Failure to manage the aircraft navigation systems and automation.
IR.VII.A.R2	2. Possible reasons for loss of communication.
IR.VII.A.R3	3. Failure to follow procedures for lost communications.
IR.VII.A.R4	4. Deviating from an IFR clearance.
Skills	The applicant demonstrates the ability to:
IR.VII.A.S1	1. Recognize a loss of communication.
IR.VII.A.S2	2. Accomplish actions to re-establish communication.
IR.VII.A.S3	3. Continue to the destination according to the flight plan or deviate from the flight plan when appropriate.
IR.VII.A.S4	4. Begin an approach at the appropriate time.

Task B. One engine inoperative during straight-and-level flight and turns (AMEL, AMES)

References	14 CFR 61; FAA-H-8083-15; FAA-H-8083-3
Objective	To determine the applicant exhibits satisfactory knowledge, risk management and skills associated the procedures for operating the aircraft with an inoperative engine during straight-and-level flight and in turns.
Knowledge	The applicant demonstrates understanding of:
IR.VII.B.K1	1. The procedures and/or differences used during flight in straight-and-level flight and turns in a multiengine aircraft with one engine inoperative versus all engines operating.
Risk Management	The applicant demonstrates the ability to identify, assess and mitigate risks, encompassing:
IR.VII.B.R1	1. Manage of startle response during unexpected events.
IR.VII.B.R2	2. Failure to manage tasks with an inoperative engine.
IR.VII.B.R3	3. Failure to maintain situational awareness.
IR.VII.B.R4	4. Failure to recognize an engine failure.
IR.VII.B.R5	5. Failure to identify the correct failed engine.
IR.VII.B.R6	6. Low altitude stall/spin.
IR.VII.B.R7	7. Inability to climb or maintain altitude with an inoperative engine.
IR.VII.B.R8	8. Physiological factors when flying by reference to instruments with an inoperative engine.
Skills	The applicant demonstrates the ability to:
IR.VII.B.S1	1. Promptly recognize an engine failure simulated by the evaluator.
IR.VII.B.S2	2. Set all engine controls, reduce drag, and identify and verify the inoperative engine.
IR.VII.B.S3	3. Establish the best engine-inoperative airspeed and trims the aircraft.
IR.VII.B.S4	4. Verify the accomplishment of prescribed checklist procedures for securing the inoperative engine.
IR.VII.B.S5	5. Establish and maintain the recommended flight attitude, as necessary, for best performance during straight-and-level and turning flight.
IR.VII.B.S6	6. Attempt to determine the reason for the engine failure.
IR.VII.B.S7	7. Monitor all engine control functions and make necessary adjustments.
IR.VII.B.S8	8. Maintain the specified altitude within ±100 feet, (if within the aircraft's capability), airspeed within ±10 knots, and the specified heading within ±10°.
IR.VII.B.S9	9. Assess the aircraft's performance capability and decide an appropriate action to ensure a safe landing.
IR.VII.B.S10	10. Avoid loss of aircraft control, or attempted flight contrary to the engine-inoperative operating limitations of the aircraft.

Task C. One Engine Inoperative – Instrument Approach (AMEL, AMES)

References	14 CFR parts 61,91; FAA-H-8083-3, FAA-H-8083-15
Objective	To determine the applicant exhibits satisfactory knowledge, risk management, and skills associated with performing an instrument approach in a multiengine aircraft with an inoperative engine.
Knowledge	The applicant demonstrates understanding of:
IR.VII.C.K1	1. The procedures and/or differences used during an instrument approach in a multiengine aircraft with one engine inoperative versus all engines operating.
Risk Management	The applicant demonstrates the ability to identify, assess and mitigate risks, encompassing:
IR.VII.C.R1	1. Manage of startle response during unexpected events.
IR.VII.C.R2	2. Executing a missed approach with an inoperative engine.
IR.VII.C.R3	3. Failure to use vertical guidance, if available, during the approach.
IR.VII.C.R4	4. Failure to manage tasks with an inoperative engine.
IR.VII.C.R5	5. Failure to maintain situational awareness.
IR.VII.C.R6	6. Failure to identify the correct failed engine.
IR.VII.C.R7	7. Low altitude stall/spin.
IR.VII.C.R8	8. Inability to maintain altitude with an inoperative engine.
IR.VII.C.R9	9. Physiological factors when flying by reference to instruments with an inoperative engine.
IR.VII.C.R10	10. Failure to manage the aircraft automation.
Skills	The applicant demonstrates the ability to:
IR.VII.C.S1	1. Promptly recognize an engine failure simulated by the evaluator.
IR.VII.C.S2	2. Set all engine controls, reduce drag, and identify and verify the inoperative engine. (Simulated)
IR.VII.C.S3	3. Establish the best engine-inoperative airspeed or airspeed appropriate for the phase of flight, and trim the aircraft.
IR.VII.C.S4	4. Attempt to determine the reason for the engine failure.
IR.VII.C.S5	5. Accomplish prescribed checklist procedures for securing the inoperative engine. (Simulated)
IR.VII.C.S6	6. Establish and maintain the recommended flight attitude and configuration for the best performance during the instrument approach procedures.
IR.VII.C.S7	7. Monitor all engine control functions and make necessary adjustments.
IR.VII.C.S8	8. Follow the actual or a simulated ATC clearance for a straight-in or circling instrument approach.
IR.VII.C.S9	9. Establish a rate of descent that will ensure arrival at the MDA/DA prior to reaching the MAP with the aircraft continuously in a position from which descent to a landing on the intended runway can be made.
IR.VII.C.S10	10. Maintain, where applicable, the specified altitude within ±100 feet, the airspeed within ±10 knots if within the aircraft's capability, and the heading within ±10°.
IR.VII.C.S11	11. Set the navigation and communication equipment used during the approach and use the proper communications technique.
IR.VII.C.S12	12. Avoid loss of aircraft control or flight contrary to the engine- inoperative operating limitations of the aircraft.

(continued...)

(...continued)

Task C. One Engine Inoperative – Instrument Approach (AMEL, AMES)

IR.VII.C.S13	13. Use a MFD and other graphical navigation displays, if installed, to monitor position and track to help navigate the approach.
IR.VII.C.S14	14. Comply with the published minima for the approach.
IR.VII.C.S15	15. During the final approach, allow no more than ¾-scale deflection (precision approach) of either the localizer or glideslope or GPS indications, or within ±10° or ¾-scale deflection during a non-precision approach.
IR.VII.C.S16	16. Assess aircraft performance capability and decide appropriate action to ensure a safe landing.

Task D. Approach with Loss of Primary Flight Instrument Indicators

References	14 CFR parts 61, 91; FAA-H-8083-15; IAP
Objective	To determine the applicant exhibits satisfactory knowledge, risk management, and skills associated with performing an approach with the loss of primary flight control instruments.
Knowledge	The applicant demonstrates understanding of:
IR.VII.D.K1	1. Common failure modes of vacuum and electric attitude instruments.
IR.VII.D.K2	2. Recognizing and confirming likely malfunctions, and how to correct or minimize the effect of their loss.
Risk Management	The applicant demonstrates the ability to identify, assess and mitigate risks, encompassing:
IR.VII.D.R1	1. Use of secondary flight displays when primary displays have failed.
IR.VII.D.R2	2. Failure to maintain situational awareness.
IR.VII.D.R3	3. Failure to follow prescribed procedures.
IR.VII.D.R4	4. Excessive descent rates.
IR.VII.D.R5	5. Deteriorating weather conditions on approach.
IR.VII.D.R6	6. An unstable approach.
IR.VII.D.R7	7. Failure to ensure proper aircraft configuration during an approach and missed approach.
IR.VII.D.R8	8. Descending below the MDA without proper visual references.
IR.VII.D.R9	9. Failure to manage the aircraft automation.
Skills	The applicant demonstrates the ability to:
IR.VII.D.S1	1. Advise ATC or evaluator if unable to comply with a clearance.
IR.VII.D.S2	2. Complete a nonprecision instrument approach without the use of the primary flight instruments using the skill elements of the Nonprecision approach Task. (See Area of Operation VI, Task A)

VIII. Postflight Procedures

Task A. Checking Instruments and Equipment

References	14 CFR parts 61, 91
Objective	To determine the applicant exhibits satisfactory knowledge, risk management, and skills associated with checking flight instruments and equipment during postflight.
Knowledge	The applicant demonstrates understanding of:
IR.VIII.A.K1	1. Documenting equipment malfunctions.
IR.VIII.A.K2	2. Aircraft accident/incident reporting.
Risk Management	The applicant demonstrates the ability to identify, assess and mitigate risks, encompassing:
IR.VIII.A.R1	1. Failure to perform a proper post-flight inspection.
IR.VIII.A.R2	2. Failure to properly document aircraft discrepancies.
Skills	The applicant demonstrates the ability to:
IR.VIII.A.S1	1. Check all flight equipment for proper operation.
IR.VIII.A.S2	2. Note all equipment and/or aircraft malfunctions and make appropriate documentation of the improper operation or failure of such equipment.

Appendix Table of Contents

Appendix 1: The Knowledge Test Eligibility, Prerequisites and Testing Centers

Knowledge Test Description

The knowledge test is an important part of the airman certification process. Applicants must pass the knowledge test before taking the practical test.

The knowledge test consists of objective, multiple-choice questions. There is a single correct response for each test question. Each test question is independent of other questions. A correct response to one question does not depend upon, or influence, the correct response to another.

Knowledge Test Tables

Test Code	Test Name	Number of Questions	Age	Allotted Time	Passing Score
AIF	Flight Instructor Instrument Airplane **(Added Rating)***	20	16	1.0	70
FIH	Flight Instructor Instrument Helicopter	50	16	2.5	70
FII	Flight Instructor Instrument Airplane	50	16	2.5	70
HIF	Flight Instructor Instrument Helicopter **(Added Rating)***	20	16	1.0	70
ICH	Instrument Rating Helicopter *Canadian Conversion*	40	15	2.0	70
ICP	Instrument Rating Airplane *Canadian Conversion*	40	15	2.0	70
IFP	Instrument Rating Foreign Pilot	50	N/A	2.5	70
IGI	Ground Instructor Instrument	50	16	2.5	70
IRA	Instrument Rating Airplane	60	15	2.5	70
IRH	Instrument Rating Helicopter	60	15	2.5	70

*See Rating Table Appendix 4

Knowledge Test Blueprint

IRA Knowledge Areas Required by 14 CFR §61.65 to be on the Knowledge Test	Percent of Questions Per Test
I. Regulations	5 - 15%
II. IFR En Route and Approach Procedures	5 - 15%
III. Air Traffic Control and Procedures	5 - 20%
IV. IFR Navigation	5 - 20%
V. Weather Reports, Critical Weather, Wind shear and Forecasts	10 - 20%
VI. Safe, Efficient IFR Operations	5 - 15%
VII. Aeronautical Decision Making	5 - 10%
VIII. Crew Resource Management	5 - 10%
Total Number of Questions	**60**

English Language Proficiency

In accordance with the requirements of 14 CFR part 61 and the FAA Aviation English Language Proficiency standard, throughout the application and testing process the applicant must demonstrate the ability to read, write, speak, and understand the English language. English language proficiency is required to communicate effectively with ATC, to comply with ATC instructions, and to ensure clear and effective crew communication and coordination. Normal restatement of questions as would be done for a native English speaker is permitted, and does not constitute grounds for disqualification.

Knowledge Test Requirements

In order to take the Instrument Rating knowledge test, you must provide proper identification. To verify your eligibility to take the test, you must also provide one of the following in accordance with the requirements of 14 CFR part 61:

- Section 61.35 lists the prerequisites for taking the knowledge test, to include the minimum age an applicant must be to sit for the test.

  Received an endorsement, if required by this part, from an authorized instructor certifying that the applicant accomplished the appropriate ground-training or a home-study course required by this part for the certificate or rating sought and is prepared for the knowledge test;

  Proper identification at the time of application that contains the applicant's—

  - (i) Photograph;
  - (ii) Signature;
  - (iii) Date of birth;
  - (iv) If the permanent mailing address is a post office box number, then the applicant must provide a government-issued residential address

- Section 61.49 acceptable forms of retest authorization for **all** Instrument Rating tests:

  An applicant retesting **after failure** is required to submit the applicable test report indicating failure, along with an endorsement from an authorized instructor who gave the applicant the required additional training. The endorsement must certify that the applicant is competent to pass the test. The test proctor must retain the original failed test report presented as authorization and attach it to the applicable sign-in/out log.

  > **Note:** If the applicant no longer possesses the original test report, he or she may request a duplicate replacement issued by AFS-760.

- Acceptable forms of authorization for Instrument Rating Airplane Canadian Conversion (ICP) only:

  Confirmation of Verification Letter issued by the Airman Certification Branch (Knowledge Testing Authorization Requirements Matrix).

  Requires **no** instructor endorsement or other form of written authorization.

Knowledge Test Centers

The FAA authorizes hundreds of knowledge testing center locations that offer a full range of airman knowledge tests. For information on authorized testing centers and to register for the knowledge test, contact one of the providers listed at www.faa.gov.

Knowledge Test Registration

When you contact a knowledge testing center to register for a test, please be prepared to select a test date, choose a testing center, and make financial arrangements for test payment when you call. You may register for test(s) several weeks in advance, and you may cancel in accordance with the testing center's cancellation policy.

Appendix 2: Knowledge Test Procedures and Tips

Before starting the actual test, the testing center will provide an opportunity to practice navigating through the test. This practice or tutorial session may include sample questions to familiarize the applicant with the look and feel of the software. (e.g., selecting an answer, marking a question for later review, monitoring time remaining for the test, and other features of the testing software.)

Acceptable Materials

The applicant may use the following aids, reference materials, and test materials, as long as the material does not include actual test questions or answers:

Acceptable Materials	Unacceptable Materials	Notes
Supplement book provided by proctor	Written materials that are handwritten, printed, or electronic	Testing centers may provide calculators and/or deny the use of personal calculators
All models of aviation-oriented calculators or small electronic calculators that perform only arithmetic functions	Electronic calculators incorporating permanent or continuous type memory circuits without erasure capability	Unit Member (proctor) may prohibit the use of your calculator if he or she is unable to determine the calculator's erasure capability
Calculators with simple programmable memories, which allow addition to, subtraction from, or retrieval of one number from the memory; or simple functions, such as square root and percentages	Magnetic Cards, magnetic tapes, modules, computer chips, or any other device upon which pre-written programs or information related to the test can be stored and retrieved	Printouts of data must be surrendered at the completion of the test if the calculator incorporates this design feature
Scales, straightedges, protractors, plotters, navigation computers, blank log sheets, holding pattern entry aids, and electronic or mechanical calculators that are directly related to the test	Dictionaries	Before, and upon completion of the test, while in the presence of the Unit Member, actuate the ON/OFF switch or RESET button, and perform any other function that ensures erasure of any data stored in memory circuits
Manufacturer's permanently inscribed instructions on the front and back of such aids, e.g., formulas, conversions, regulations, signals, weather data, holding pattern diagrams, frequencies, weight and balance formulas, and air traffic control procedures	Any booklet or manual containing instructions related to use of test aids	Unit Member makes the final determination regarding aids, reference materials, and test materials

Test Tips

When taking a knowledge test, please keep the following points in mind:

- Carefully read the instructions provided with the test.

- Answer each question in accordance with the latest regulations and guidance publications.

- Read each question carefully before looking at the answer options. You should clearly understand the problem before trying to solve it.

- After formulating a response, determine which answer option corresponds with your answer. The answer you choose should completely solve the problem.

- Remember that only one answer is complete and correct. The other possible answers are either incomplete or erroneous.

- If a certain question is difficult for you, mark it for review and return to it after you have answered the less difficult questions. This procedure will enable you to use the available time to maximum advantage.

- When solving a calculation problem, be sure to read all the associated notes.

- For questions involving use of a graph, you may request a printed copy that you can mark in computing your answer. This copy and all other notes and paperwork must be given to the testing center upon completion of the test.

Cheating or Other Unauthorized Conduct

To avoid test compromise, computer testing centers must follow strict security procedures established by the FAA and described in FAA Order 8080.6 (as amended), Conduct of Airman Knowledge Tests. The FAA has directed testing centers to terminate a test at any time a test unit member suspects that a cheating incident has occurred.

The FAA will investigate and, if the agency determines that cheating or unauthorized conduct has occurred, any airman certificate or rating you hold may be revoked. You will also be prohibited from applying for or taking any test for a certificate or rating under 14 CFR part 61 for a period of one year.

Testing Procedures for Applicants Requesting Special Accommodations

An applicant with learning or reading disability may request approval from AFS-630 through the local Flight Standards District Office (FSDO) or International Field Office/International Field Unit (IFO/IFU) to take airman knowledge test using one of the three options listed below, in preferential order:

Option 1: Use current testing facilities and procedures whenever possible.

Option 2: Use a self-contained, electronic device which pronounces and displays typed-in words (e.g., the Franklin Speaking Wordmaster®) to facilitate the testing process.

> **Note:** *The device should consist of an electronic thesaurus that audibly pronounces typed-in words and presents them on a display screen. The device should also have a built-in headphone jack in order to avoid disturbing others during testing.*

Option 3: Request the proctor's assistance in reading specific words or terms from the test questions and/or supplement book. To prevent compromising the testing process, the proctor must be an individual with no aviation background or expertise. The proctor may provide reading assistance only (i.e., no explanation of words or terms). When an applicant requests this option, the FSDO or IFO/IFU inspector must contact the Airman Testing Standards Branch (AFS-630) for assistance in selecting the test site and assisting the proctor. Before approving any option, the FSDO or IFO/IFU inspector must advise the applicant of the regulatory certification requirement to be able to read, write, speak, and understand the English language.

Appendix 3: Airman Knowledge Test Report

Immediately upon completion of the knowledge test, the applicant receives a printed Airman Knowledge Test Report documenting the score with the testing center's raised, embossed seal. The applicant must retain the original Airman Knowledge Test Report. The instructor must provide instruction in each area of deficiency and provide a logbook endorsement certifying that the applicant has demonstrated satisfactory knowledge in each area. When taking the practical test, the applicant must present the original Airman Knowledge Test Report to the evaluator, who is required to assess the noted areas of deficiency during the ground portion of the practical test.

An Airman Knowledge Test Report expires 24 calendar months after the month the applicant completes the knowledge test. If the Airman Knowledge Test Report expires before completion of the practical test, the applicant must retake the knowledge test.

To obtain a duplicate Airman Knowledge Test Report due to loss or destruction of the original, the applicant can send a signed request accompanied by a check or money order for $12.00 (U.S. funds), payable to the FAA to:

> Federal Aviation Administration
> Airmen Certification Branch, AFS-760
> P.O. Box 25082
> Oklahoma City, OK 73125

To obtain a copy of the application form or a list of the information required, please see the Airman Certification Branch (AFS-760) web page.

FAA Knowledge Test Question Coding

Each Task in the Airman Certification Standard includes an Airman Certification Standards (ACS) code. This ACS code will soon be displayed on the airman test report to indicate what Task element was proven deficient on the Knowledge Exam. Instructors can then provide remedial training in the deficient areas and evaluators can re-test this element during the practical exam.

The ACS coding consists of four elements. For example: this code is interpreted as follows:

> IR.I.C.K1:
>   IR = Applicable ACS (Instrument Rating – Airplane)
>   I   = Area of Operation (Preflight Preparation)
>   C   = Task (Cross-Country Flight Planning)
>   K1 = Task Element Knowledge 1 (Fuel planning)

Knowledge test questions are mapped to the ACS codes, which will soon replace the system of "Learning Statement Codes." After this transition occurs, the airman knowledge test report will list an ACS code that correlates to a specific Task element for a given Area of Operation and Task. Remedial instruction and re-testing will be specific, targeted, and based on specified learning criteria. Similarly, a Notice of Disapproval for the practical test will use the ACS codes to identify the deficient Task elements.

Appendix 4: The Practical Test – Eligibility and Prerequisites

The prerequisite requirements and general eligibility for a practical test and the specific requirements for the original issuance of an instrument rating in the airplane can be found in 14 CFR sections 61.39 and 61.65, respectively.

Additional Instrument Rating Desired

If you hold an instrument rating in another category and adding Instrument – Airplane, you are required to complete the Task(s) indicated in the following table:

Area of Operation	Required Task(s)
I	None
II	A,C
III	None
IV	All
V	None
VI	All
VII	All[1]
VIII	All

1 TASK B and C are applicable *only to multiengine airplanes*

Appendix 5: Practical Test Roles, Responsibilities, and Outcomes

Applicant Responsibilities

The applicant is responsible for mastering the established standards for knowledge, risk management, and skill elements in all Tasks appropriate to the certificate and rating sought. The applicant should use this ACS, its references, and the Applicant's Practical Test Checklist in this Appendix in preparation to take the practical test.

Instructor Responsibilities

The instructor is responsible for training the applicant to meet the established standards for knowledge, risk management, and skill elements in all Tasks appropriate to the certificate and rating sought. The instructor should use this ACS and its references as part of preparing the applicant to take the practical test and, if necessary, in retraining the applicant to proficiency in all subject(s) missed on the knowledge test.

Evaluator Responsibilities

An Evaluator is:

- Aviation safety inspector (ASI)

- Pilot examiner (other than administrative pilot examiners) or

- Chief instructor, assistant chief instructor or check instructor of pilot school holding examining authority

- CFII conducting an IPC

The evaluator who conducts the practical test is responsible for determining that the applicant meets the established standards of aeronautical knowledge, skills (flight proficiency), and risk management for each Task in the appropriate ACS. This responsibility also includes verifying the experience requirements specified for a certificate or rating.

At the initial stage of the practical test, the evaluator must also determine that the applicant meets FAA Aviation English Language Proficiency (AELP) standards by verifying that he or she can understand ATC instructions and communicate in English at a level that is understandable to ATC and other pilots. The evaluator should use AC 60-28, English Language Skill Standards required by 14 CFR parts 61, 63, and 65 (current version) when evaluating the applicant's ability to meet the standard. If, at any point during the practical test, the applicant does not meet the AELP standards, the evaluator must issue a Notice of Disapproval, FAA form 8060-5, with "NOT FAA AELP" in the comments. If there is any doubt, the evaluator should contact the local Flight Standards District Office (FSDO) for assistance.

The evaluator must develop a Plan of Action (POA), written in English, to conduct the practical test. It must include all of the required Areas of Operation and Tasks. The POA must include a scenario that evaluates as many of the required Areas of Operation and Tasks as possible. As the scenario unfolds during the test, the evaluator will introduce problems and emergencies that the applicant must manage. The evaluator has the discretion to modify the POA in order to accommodate unexpected situations as they arise. For example, the evaluator may elect to suspend and later resume a scenario in order to assess certain Tasks.

In the integrated ACS framework, the Areas of Operation contain Tasks that include "knowledge" elements (such as K1), "risk management" elements (such as R1), and "skill" elements (such as S1). Knowledge and risk management elements are primarily evaluated during the knowledge testing phase of the airman certification process. The evaluator must assess the applicant on all Skill elements for each Task included in each Area of Operation of the ACS, unless otherwise noted. The evaluator administering the practical test has the discretion to combine Tasks/elements as appropriate to testing scenarios.

- The required minimum elements to include in the POA from each applicable Task are as follows:

    o At least one knowledge element;

    o At least one risk management element;

    o All skill elements unless otherwise noted; and

    o Any Task elements in which the applicant was shown to be deficient on the knowledge test.

> **Note:** *Task elements added to the POA on the basis of being listed on the AKTR may satisfy the other minimum Task element requirements. The missed items on the AKTR are not required to be added in addition to the minimum Task element requirements.*

There is no expectation for testing every knowledge element and risk management element in a Task, but the evaluator has discretion to sample as needed to ensure the applicant's mastery of that Task.

Unless otherwise noted in the Task, the evaluator must test each item in the skills section by asking the applicant to perform each one. As safety of flight conditions permit, the evaluator may use questions during flight to test knowledge and risk management elements not evident in the demonstrated skills. To the greatest extent practicable, evaluators shall test the applicant's ability to apply and correlate information, and use rote questions only when they are appropriate for the material being tested. If the Task includes sub-elements (such as IR.VI.B.S7a NOTAMs), the evaluator may select either the primary element (such as S7) or an appropriate sub-element (such as S7a). If the broader primary element is selected, the evaluator must develop questions only from material covered in the references listed for the Task.

Possible Outcomes of the Test

There are three possible outcomes of the practical test: (1) Temporary Airman Certificate (satisfactory), (2) Notice of Disapproval (unsatisfactory), or (3) Letter of Discontinuance.

If the evaluator determines that a Task is incomplete, or the outcome is uncertain, the evaluator may require the applicant to repeat that Task, or portions of that Task. This provision does not mean that instruction, practice, or the repetition of an unsatisfactory Task is permitted during the practical test.

If the evaluator determines the applicant's skill and abilities are in doubt, the outcome is unsatisfactory and the evaluator must issue a Notice of Disapproval.

Satisfactory Performance

Satisfactory performance requires that the applicant:

- Demonstrate the Tasks specified in the Areas of Operation for the certificate or rating sought within the established standards;

- Demonstrate mastery of the aircraft by performing each Task successfully;

- Demonstrate proficiency and competency in accordance with the approved standards;

- Demonstrate sound judgment and exercise aeronautical decision-making/risk management;

- Demonstrate competence in crew resource management in aircraft certificated for more than one required pilot crew member, or, single-pilot competence in an airplane that is certificated for single-pilot operations.

Satisfactory performance will result in the issuance of a temporary certificate.

Unsatisfactory Performance

If, in the judgment of the evaluator, the applicant does not meet the standards for any Task, the applicant fails the Task and associated Area of Operation. The test is unsatisfactory, and the evaluator issues a Notice of Disapproval.

When the evaluator issues a Notice of Disapproval, he or she shall list the ACS code associated with the Area of Operation in which the application did not meet the standard. The Notice of Disapproval must also list the Area(s) of Operation not tested, and the number of practical test failures.

The evaluator or the applicant may end the test if the applicant fails a Task. The evaluator may continue the test only with the consent of the applicant, and the applicant is entitled to credit only those Areas of Operation and the associated Tasks satisfactorily performed. Though not required, the evaluator has discretion to reevaluate any Task, including those previously passed, during the retest.

Typical areas of unsatisfactory performance and grounds for disqualification include:

- Any action or lack of action by the applicant that requires corrective intervention by the evaluator to maintain safe flight.

- Failure to use proper and effective visual scanning techniques to clear the area before and while performing maneuvers.

- Consistently exceeding tolerances stated in the skill elements of the Task.

- Failure to take prompt corrective action when tolerances are exceeded.

- Failure to exercise risk management.

Discontinuance

When it is necessary to issue a Letter of Discontinuance of the discontinuance to the practical test for reasons other than unsatisfactory performance (e.g., equipment failure, weather, illness), the evaluator must return all test paperwork to the applicant. The evaluator must prepare, sign, and issue a Letter of Discontinuance that lists those Areas of Operation the applicant successfully completed and the date the test must be completed. The evaluator should advise the applicant to present the Letter of Discontinuance to the evaluator when the practical test resumes in order to receive credit for the items successfully completed. The Letter of Discontinuance becomes part of the applicant's certification file.

Practical Test Checklist (Applicant)

Appointment with Evaluator

Evaluator's Name: _____

Location: _____

Date/Time: _____

Acceptable Aircraft

- ☐ Aircraft Documents:
    - ☐ Airworthiness Certificate
    - ☐ Registration Certificate
    - ☐ Operating Limitations
- ☐ Aircraft Maintenance Records:
    - ☐ Logbook Record of Airworthiness Inspections and AD Compliance
- ☐ Pilot's Operating Handbook, FAA-Approved Aircraft Flight Manual

Personal Equipment

- ☐ View-Limiting Device
- ☐ Current Aeronautical Charts (May be electronic)
- ☐ Computer and Plotter
- ☐ Flight Plan Form
- ☐ Flight Plan Form and Flight Logs (printed or electronic)
- ☐ Chart Supplements, U.S., Airport Diagrams and Appropriate Publications (regulations, AIM, etc.)

Personal Records

- ☐ Identification—Photo/Signature ID
- ☐ Pilot Certificate
- ☐ Current Medical Certificate
- ☐ Completed FAA Form 8710-1, Airman Certificate and/or Rating Application with Instructor's Signature
- ☐ Original Knowledge Test Report
- ☐ Pilot Logbook with appropriate Instructor Endorsements
- ☐ FAA Form 8060-5, Notice of Disapproval (if applicable)
- ☐ Letter of Discontinuance (if applicable)
- ☐ Approved School Graduation Certificate (if applicable)
- ☐ Evaluator's Fee (if applicable)

Instrument Proficiency Check

Section 61.57(d) sets forth the requirements for an instrument proficiency check (IPC). Instructors and evaluators conducting an IPC must ensure the pilot meets the standards established in this ACS. A representative number of Tasks must be selected to assure the competence of the applicant to operate in the IFR environment. As a minimum, the applicant must demonstrate the ability to perform the Tasks listed in the table below. The person giving the check should develop a scenario that incorporates as many required Tasks as practical to assess the pilot's ADM and risk management skills.

Guidance on how to conduct an IPC is found in Advisory Circular 61-98, *Currency Requirements and Guidance for the Flight Review and Instrument Proficiency Check*. You may obtain a copy at: http://www.faa.gov.

Area of Operation	IPC (Proficiency Check)[2]
I	None
II	None
III	B
IV	B
V	A
VI	All
VII[3]	B, C, D
VIII	All

2 AATDs can be utilized for the majority of the IPC as specified in the Letter of Authorization issued for the device. However, the circling approach, the landing Task, and the multiengine airplane Tasks must be accomplished in an aircraft or FFS (Level B, C, or D).

3 Task B and C are applicable *only to multiengine airplanes.*

Appendix 6: Safety of Flight

General

Safety of flight must be the prime consideration at all times. The evaluator, applicant, and crew must be constantly alert for other traffic. If performing aspects of a given maneuver, such as emergency procedures, would jeopardize safety, the evaluator will ask the applicant to simulate that portion of the maneuver. The evaluator will assess the applicant's use of visual scanning and collision avoidance procedures throughout the entire test.

Stall and Spin Awareness

During flight training and testing, the applicant and the instructor or evaluator must always recognize and avoid operations that could lead to an inadvertent stall or spin.

Use of Checklists

Throughout the practical test, the applicant is evaluated on the use of an appropriate checklist.

Assessing proper checklist use depends upon the specific Task. In all cases, the evaluator should determine whether the applicant appropriately divides attention and uses proper visual scanning. In some situations, reading the actual checklist may be impractical or unsafe. In such cases, the evaluator should assess the applicant's performance of published or recommended immediate action "memory" items along with his or her review of the appropriate checklist once conditions permit.

In a single-pilot airplane, the applicant should demonstrate the CRM principles described as single pilot resource management (SRM). Proper use is dependent on the specific Task being evaluated. The situation may be such that the use of the checklist while accomplishing elements of an Objective would be either unsafe or impractical in a single-pilot operation. In this case, a review of the checklist after the elements have been accomplished is appropriate. Use of a checklist should also consider visual scanning and division of attention at all times.

Use of Distractions

Numerous studies indicate that many accidents have occurred when the pilot has been distracted during critical phases of flight. The evaluator should incorporate realistic distractions during the flight portion of the practical test to evaluate the pilot's situational awareness and ability to utilize proper control technique while dividing attention both inside and outside the cockpit.

Positive Exchange of Flight Controls

There must always be a clear understanding of who has control of the aircraft. Prior to flight, the pilots involved should conduct a briefing that includes reviewing the procedures for exchanging flight controls.

The FAA recommends a positive three-step process for exchanging flight controls between pilots:

- When one pilot seeks to have the other pilot take control of the aircraft, he or she will say, "You have the flight controls."

- The second pilot acknowledges immediately by saying, "I have the flight controls."

- The first pilot again says, "You have the flight controls."

Pilots should follow this procedure during any exchange of flight controls, including any occurrence during the practical test. The FAA also recommends that both pilots use a visual check to verify that the exchange has occurred. There must never be any doubt as to who is flying the aircraft.

Aeronautical Decision Making, Risk Management, CRM and SRM

Throughout the practical test, the evaluator must assess the applicant's ability to use sound aeronautical decision making procedures in order to identify hazards and mitigate risk. The evaluator must accomplish this requirement by reference to the risk management elements of the given Task(s), and by developing scenarios that incorporate and combine Tasks appropriate to assessing the applicant's risk management in making safe aeronautical decisions. For example, the evaluator may develop a scenario that incorporates weather decisions and performance planning.

In assessing the applicant's performance, the evaluator should take note of the applicant's use of CRM and, if appropriate, Single Pilot Resource Management (SRM). CRM/SRM is the set of competencies that includes situational awareness, communication skills, teamwork, task allocation, and decision making within a comprehensive framework of standard operating procedures (SOP). SRM specifically refers to the management of all resources onboard the aircraft as well as outside resources available to the single pilot.

Deficiencies in CRM/SRM almost always contribute to the unsatisfactory performance of a Task. While evaluation of CRM/SRM may appear to be somewhat subjective, the evaluator should use the risk management elements of the given Task(s) to determine whether the applicant's performance of the Task(s) demonstrates both understanding and application of the associated risk management elements.

Multiengine Considerations

For multiengine practical tests conducted in the airplane, the evaluator must discuss with the applicant during the required preflight briefing the methods for simulating an engine failure in accordance with the aircraft manufacturer's recommended procedures.

For safety reasons, the applicant should perform Tasks that require feathering or engine shutdown only under environmental conditions, and in a position and altitude, where it is possible to make a safe landing on an established airport. The minimum altitude selected must allow recovery to be safely completed at a minimum of 3,000 feet AGL for nontransport category airplanes and 5,000 feet AGL for transport category airplanes. For one engine inoperative Tasks below 3,000 feet AGL (or 5,000 AGL for transport category airplanes), the evaluator must simulate an engine failure by adjusting the engine controls according to the aircraft manufacturers' recommendations to simulate zero thrust.

If there is difficulty in unfeathering the propeller or restarting the engine or if it is not possible to unfeather the propeller or restart the engine while airborne, the applicant and the evaluator should treat the situation as an emergency.

Practical tests conducted in a FSTD can only be accomplished as part of an approved curriculum or training program. Any limitations on powerplant failure will be noted in that program.

VII. Emergency Operations- One Engine Inoperative –Multiengine Airplane

In a multiengine airplane or FSTD equipped with propellers (including turboprop), the applicant must demonstrate feathering one propeller and engine shutdown unless:

- The practical test is for a type rating, and

- The airplane used for the practical test was not certificated with inflight unfeathering capability.

In this situation, the applicant may perform a simulated powerplant failure. In all other cases, the applicant must demonstrate the ability to safely feather the propeller while airborne.

In a multiengine turbojet airplane or FSTD representing a turbojet airplane, the applicant must demonstrate the shutdown of one engine while airborne.

Appendix 7: Aircraft, Equipment, and Operational Requirements & Limitations

Aircraft Requirements & Limitations

Section 61.45 prescribes the required aircraft and equipment for a practical test. The regulation states the minimum aircraft registration and airworthiness requirements as well as the minimum equipment requirements, to include the minimum required controls.

Multiengine practical tests require normal engine shutdowns and restarts in the air, to include propeller feathering and unfeathering. The AFM must not prohibit these procedures, but low power settings for cooling periods prior to the actual shutdown in accordance with the AFM are acceptable and encouraged. For a type rating in an airplane not certificated with inflight unfeathering capability, a simulated powerplant failure is acceptable.

If the multiengine airplane used for the practical test does not publish a V_{MC}, then the "Limited to Centerline Thrust" limitation will be added to the certificate issued from this check, unless the applicant has already demonstrated competence in a multiengine airplane with a published V_{MC}.

Any equipment inoperative in an aircraft with a minimum equipment list (MEL) shall be placarded in accordance with 14 CFR section 91.213 and any approved MEL procedures. The applicant shall describe the procedures accomplished, the resulting operational restrictions, and the documentation for the inoperative item(s).

Equipment Requirements & Limitations

The equipment examination should be administered before the flight portion of the practical test, but it must be closely coordinated and related to the flight portion. In a training core curriculum that has been approved under 14 CFR part 142, the evaluator may accept written evidence of the equipment exam, provided that the Administrator has approved the exam and authorized the individual who administers it.

Consistent with 14 CFR section 61.45(b) and (d), the aircraft must have

- the flight instruments necessary for controlling the aircraft without outside references,
- the radio equipment required for ATC communications, and
- the ability to perform instrument approach procedures.

GPS equipment must be instrument certified and contain the current database.

To assist in management of the aircraft during the practical test, the applicant is expected to demonstrate automation management skills by utilizing installed equipment such as autopilot, avionics and systems displays, and/or flight management system (FMS). The evaluator is expected to test the applicant's knowledge of the systems that are installed and operative during both the oral and flight portions of the practical test.

If the practical test is conducted in an aircraft, the applicant is required by 14 CFR section 61.45(d) (2) to provide an appropriate view limiting device acceptable to the evaluator. The applicant and the evaluator should establish a procedure as to when and how this device should be donned and removed, and brief this procedure before the flight. The device must be used during all testing that requires flight "solely by reference to instruments." This device must prevent the applicant from having visual reference outside the aircraft, but it must not restrict the evaluator's ability to see and avoid other traffic.

Operational Requirements & Limitations

Instrument Approach Procedures – General

A stabilized approach is characterized by a constant angle, constant rate of descent approach profile ending near the touchdown point, where the landing maneuver begins.

If the practical test is conducted in the airplane and the airplane has a properly installed and operable GPS, the applicant must demonstrate GPS approach proficiency. If the applicant has contracted for training in an approved course that includes GPS training, and the airplane/FSTD has a properly installed and operable GPS, the applicant must demonstrate GPS approach proficiency.

Localizer performance with vertical guidance (LPV) minimums with a decision altitude (DA) greater than 300 feet height above touchdown (HAT) may be used as a nonprecision approach; however, due to the precision of its glidepath and localizer-like lateral navigation characteristics, an LPV minimums can be used to demonstrate precision approach proficiency (AOO VI Task B) if the DA is equal to or less than 300 feet HAT.

The standard is to allow no more than a ¾ scale deflection of either the glideslope or localizer indications during the final approach. As the markings on localizer/glideslope indicators vary, a ¾ scale deflection of either the localizer or glideslope indicator is deemed to occur when it is displaced three-fourths of the distance that it may be deflected from the on glideslope or on localizer position.

Instrument Approach Procedures – Nonprecision Approach

The evaluator will select nonprecision approaches representative of the type that the applicant is likely to use. The choices must use at least two different types of navigational aids.

Examples of acceptable Nonprecision approaches include: VOR, LOC procedures on an ILS, LDA, RNAV (RNP) or RNAV (GPS) to LNAV, LNAV/VNAV or LPV line of minima as long as the LPV DA is greater than 300 feet HAT. The equipment must be installed and the database must be current and qualified to fly GPS-based approaches.

Practical test requirements for nonprecision approaches are as follows:

- The applicant must accomplish at least two nonprecision approaches in simulated or actual weather conditions.

   One must include a procedure turn or, in the case of a GPS-based approach, a Terminal Arrival Area (TAA) procedure.

   At least one must be flown without the use of autopilot and without the assistance of radar vectors. The yaw damper and flight director are not considered parts of the autopilot for purposes of this Task.

   If the equipment allows, at least one should be conducted without vertical guidance.

   One is expected to be flown with reference to backup or partial panel instrumentation or navigation display, depending on the aircraft's instrument avionics configuration, representing the failure mode(s) most realistic for the equipment used.

Instrument Approach Procedures – Precision Approach

The applicant must accomplish a precision approach to a decision altitude (DA) using aircraft navigational equipment for centerline and vertical guidance in simulated or actual instrument conditions. Acceptable instrument approaches for this part of the practical test are the ILS and GLS. In addition, if the installed equipment and database is current and qualified for IFR flight and approaches to LPV minima, an LPV minima approach can be flown to demonstrate precision approach proficiency if the LPV DA is equal to or less than 300 feet HAT.

In a multiengine airplane, the applicant must accomplish at least one instrument approach with simulated failure of one powerplant. The approach may be a precision or a nonprecision approach. The simulated engine failure should occur before initiating the final approach segment and must continue to touchdown.

Appendix 8: Use of Flight Simulation Training Devices (FSTD) and Aviation Training Devices (ATD): Airplane Single-Engine, Multi Engine Land and Sea

Use of FSTDs

Section 61.4, *Qualification and approval of flight simulators and flight training devices*, states in paragraph (a) that each full flight simulator (FFS) and flight training device (FTD) used for training, and for which an airman is to receive credit to satisfy any training, testing, or checking requirement under this chapter, must be qualified and approved by the Administrator for—

(1) The training, testing, and checking for which it is used;

(2) Each particular maneuver, procedure, or crewmember function performed; and

(3) The representation of the specific category and class of aircraft, type of aircraft, particular variation within the type of aircraft, or set of aircraft for certain flight training devices.

14 CFR part 60 prescribes the rules governing the initial and continuing qualification and use of all FSTDs used for meeting training, evaluation, or flight experience requirements for flight crewmember certification or qualification.

An FSTD is defined in 14 CFR part 60 as an FFS or FTD:

Full Flight Simulator (FFS)—a replica of a specific type, make, model, or series aircraft. It includes the equipment and computer programs necessary to represent aircraft operations in ground and flight conditions, a visual system providing an out-of-the-flight deck view, a system that provides cues at least equivalent to those of a three-degree-of-freedom motion system, and has the full range of capabilities of the systems installed in the device as described in part 60 of this chapter and the QPS for a specific FFS qualification level. (part 1)

Flight Training Device (FTD)—a replica of aircraft instruments, equipment, panels, and controls in an open flight deck area or an enclosed aircraft flight deck replica. It includes the equipment and computer programs necessary to represent aircraft (or set of aircraft) operations in ground and flight conditions having the full range of capabilities of the systems installed in the device as described in part 60 of this chapter and the qualification performance standard (QPS) for a specific FTD qualification level. (part 1)

The FAA National Simulator Program (NSP) qualifies Level A-D FFSs and Level 4 – 7[4] FTDs. In addition, each operational rule part identifies additional requirements for the approval and use of FSTDs in a training program[5]. Use of an FSTD for the completion of the instrument-airplane rating practical test is permitted only when accomplished in accordance with an FAA approved curriculum or training program. Use of an FSTD for the completion of an instrument proficiency check is also permitted when accomplished in accordance with an FAA approved curriculum or training program.

---

4 The FSTD qualification standards in effect prior to part 60 defined a Level 7 FTD for airplanes (see Advisory Circular 12045A, Airplane Flight Training Device Qualification, 1992). This device required high fidelity, airplane specific aerodynamic and flight control models similar to a Level D FFS, but did not require a motion cueing system or visual display system. In accordance with the "grandfather rights" of 14 CFR section 60.17, these previously qualified devices will retain their qualification basis as long as they continue to meet the standards under which they were originally qualified. There is only one airplane Level 7 FTD with grandfather rights that remains in the U.S. As a result of changes to part 60 that were published in the Federal Register in March 2016, the airplane Level 7 FTD was reinstated with updated evaluation standards. The new Level 7 FTD will require a visual display system for qualification. The minimum qualified Tasks for the Level 7 FTD are described in Table B1B of Appendix B of part 60.

5 Section 121.407, 14 CFR section 135.335, section 141.41, and section 142.59

Use of ATDs

14 CFR part 61, (c) states the Administrator may approve a device other than an FFS or FTD for specific purposes. Under this authority, the FAA's General Aviation and Commercial Division provide approval for aviation training devices (ATD).

Advisory Circular (AC) 61136A, *FAA Approval of Aviation Training Devices and Their Use for Training and Experience*, provides information and guidance for the required function, performance, and effective use of ATDs for pilot training and aeronautical experience (including currency). FAA issues a letter of authorization (LOA) to an ATD manufacturer approving an ATD as a basic aviation training device (BATD) or an advanced aviation training device (AATD). The LOA will be valid for a five-year period with a specific expiration date and include the amount of credit a pilot may take for training and experience.

> *Aviation Training Device (ATD)—a training device, other than an FFS or FTD, that has been evaluated, qualified, and approved by the Administrator. In general, this includes a replica of aircraft instruments, equipment, panels, and controls in an open flight deck area or an enclosed aircraft cockpit. It includes the hardware and software necessary to represent a category and class of aircraft (or set of aircraft) operations in ground and flight conditions having the appropriate range of capabilities and systems installed in the device as described within the AC for the specific basic or advanced qualification level.*

> *Basic Aviation Training Device (BATD)—provides an adequate training platform for both procedural and operational performance Tasks specific to instrument experience and the ground and flight training requirements for the private pilot certificate and instrument rating per 14 CFR parts 61 and 141.*

> *Advanced Aviation Training Device (AATD)—provides an adequate training platform for both procedural and operational performance Tasks specific to the ground and flight training requirements for the private pilot certificate, instrument rating, commercial pilot certificate, airline transport pilot (ATP) certificate, and flight instructor certificate per 14 CFR parts 61 and 141. It also provides an adequate platform for Tasks required for instrument experience and the instrument proficiency check.*

ATDs cannot be used for practical tests, aircraft type specific training, or for an aircraft type rating; therefore the use of an ATD for the instrument – airplane rating practical test is not permitted. An AATD, however, may be used for some of the required Tasks of an instrument proficiency check as further explained in this appendix.

Credit for Time in an FSTD

Section 61.65 specifies the minimum aeronautical experience requirements for a person applying for an instrument rating. Paragraph (d) specifies the time requirements for an instrument-airplane rating, which includes specific experience requirements that must be completed in an airplane. Paragraph (h) of this section specifies the amount of credit a pilot can take for time in an FFS or FTD. For those that received training in programs outside of 14 CFR part 142, section 61.65(h) (2)[6] applies. For those pilots that received training through a 14 CFR part 142 program, section 61.65(h) (1) applies.

Credit for Time in an ATD

Section 61.65 specifies the minimum aeronautical experience requirements for a person applying for an instrument rating. Paragraph (d) specifies the time requirements for an instrument-airplane rating, which includes specific experience requirements that must be completed in an airplane. Paragraph (i) specifies the maximum instrument time in an ATD a pilot may credit towards the instrument rating aeronautical experience requirements. Paragraph (i) specifies the maximum instrument time a pilot may credit in any combination of a FFS, FTD, and ATD.

---

6 As part of program approval, part 141 training providers must also adhere to the requirements for permitted time in an FFS, FTD, or ATD per Appendix C to part 141.

In order to credit the time, the ATD must be FAA-approved and the instrument time must be provided by an authorized instructor. AC 61-136A, states the LOA for each approved ATD will indicate the credit allowances for pilot training and experience, as provided under parts 61 and 141. Time with an instructor in a BATD and an AATD may be credited towards the aeronautical experience requirements for the instrument-airplane rating as specified in the LOA for the device used. It is recommended that applicants who intend to take credit for time in a BATD or an AATD towards the aeronautical experience requirements for the instrument-airplane rating obtain a copy of the LOA for each device used so they have a record for how much credit may be taken. For additional information on the logging of ATD time reference AC 61-136A, see Appendix 5.

Instrument Experience

Section 61.57 provides the recent flight experience requirements to serve as a PIC. Paragraph (c) specifies the necessary instrument experience required to serve as a PIC under IFR. The experience may be gained in an airplane, an FSTD, or an ATD. Refer to the subparagraphs of 14 CFR section 61.57(c) to determine the experience needed, which varies depending upon whether an airplane, FSTD, ATD, or combination of airplane and training devices are used.

Instrument Proficiency Check

If a person fails to meet the experience requirements of 14 CFR section 61.57(c), a pilot may only establish instrument currency through an instrument proficiency check as described in 14 CFR section 61.57(d). An FSTD may be used as part of an approved curriculum to accomplish all or portions of this check. If specified in its LOA, an AATD may be used to complete most of the required Tasks. However, the circling approach, the landing Task, and the multiengine airplane Tasks must be accomplished in an aircraft or FFS (Level B, C, or D). A BATD cannot be used for an instrument proficiency check. Please see the Task Table in Appendix 5 for additional information. (Appendix 5, Instrument Proficiency Check Table).

Use of an FSTD on a Practical Test

Section 61.45 specifies the required aircraft and equipment that must be provided for a practical test unless permitted to use an FFS or FTD for the flight portion. Section 61 64 provides the criteria for using an FSTD for a practical test. Specifically, paragraph (a) states –

> If an applicant for a certificate or rating uses a flight simulator or flight training device for training or any portion of the practical test, the flight simulator and flight training device—
>
> (1) Must represent the category, class, and type (if a type rating is applicable) for the rating sought; and
>
> (2) Must be qualified and approved by the Administrator and used in accordance with an approved course of training under 14 CFR part 141 or 142 of this chapter; or under 14 CFR part 121 or 135 of this chapter, provided the applicant is a pilot employee of that air carrier operator.

Therefore, practical tests or portions thereof, when accomplished in an FSTD, may only be conducted by FAA aviation safety inspectors (ASI), aircrew program designees (APD) authorized to conduct such tests in FSTDs in 14 CFR parts 121 or 135, qualified personnel and designees authorized to conduct such tests in FSTDs for part 141 pilot school graduates, or appropriately authorized part 142 Training Center Evaluators (TCE).

In addition, 14 CFR section 61.64(b) states if an airplane is not used during the practical test for a type rating for a turbojet airplane (except for preflight inspection), an applicant must accomplish the entire practical test in a Level C or higher FFS and the applicant must meet the specific experience criteria listed. If the experience criteria cannot be met, the applicant can either—

(f)(1) [...] complete the following s on the practical test in an aircraft appropriate to category, class, and type for the rating sought: Preflight inspection, normal takeoff, normal instrument landing system approach, missed approach, and normal landing; or

(f)(2) The applicant's pilot certificate will be issued with a limitation that states: "The [name of the additional type rating] is subject to pilot in command limitations," and the applicant is restricted from serving as pilot in command in an aircraft of that type.

When flight Tasks are accomplished in an airplane, certain Task elements may be accomplished through "simulated" actions in the interest of safety and practicality. However, when accomplished in an FFS or FTD, these same actions would not be "simulated." For example, when in an airplane, a simulated engine fire may be addressed by retarding the throttle to idle, simulating the shutdown of the engine, simulating the discharge of the fire suppression agent, if applicable, and simulating the disconnection of associated electrical, hydraulic, and pneumatics systems. However, when the same emergency condition is addressed in a FSTD, all Task elements must be accomplished as would be expected under actual circumstances.

Similarly, safety of flight precautions taken in the airplane for the accomplishment of a specific maneuver or procedure (such as limiting altitude in an approach to stall or setting maximum airspeed for an engine failure expected to result in a rejected takeoff) need not be taken when a FSTD is used. It is important to understand that, whether accomplished in an airplane or FSTD, all Tasks and elements for each maneuver or procedure shall have the same performance standards applied equally for determination of overall satisfactory performance.

Appendix 9: References

This ACS is based on the following 14 CFR parts, FAA guidance documents, manufacturer's publications, and other documents.

Reference	Title
14 CFR part 61	Certification: Pilots, Flight Instructors, and Ground Instructors
14 CFR part 91	General Operating and Flight Rules
AC 00-6	Aviation Weather
AC 00-45	Aviation Weather Services
AC 60-28	English Language Skill Standards Required by 14 CFR parts 61, 63 and 65
AC 91-74	Pilot Guide: Flight in Icing Conditions
AIM	Aeronautical Information Manual
Chart Supplements U.S.	Chart Supplements U.S. (previously Airport/Facility Directory or A/FD)
FAA-H-8083-2	Risk Management Handbook
FAA-H-8083-3	Airplane Flying Handbook
FAA-H-8083-15	Instrument Flying Handbook
FAA-H-8083-16	Instrument Procedures Handbook
FAA-H-8083-25	Pilot's Handbook of Aeronautical Knowledge
IAP	Instrument Approach Procedures
POH/AFM	Pilot's Operating Handbook/FAA-Approved Airplane Flight Manual
Other	NOTAMs

Note: *Users should reference the current edition of the reference documents listed above. The current edition of all FAA publications can be found at www.faa.gov.*

Appendix 10: Abbreviations and Acronyms

The following abbreviations and acronyms are used in the ACS.

Abb./Acronym	Definition
14 CFR	Title 14 of the Code of Federal Regulations
AATD	Advanced Aviation Training Device
AC	Advisory Circular
ACS	Airman Certification Standards
AD	Airworthiness Directive
ADF	Automatic Direction Finder
ADM	Aeronautical Decision-Making
AFS	Flight Standards Service
AELP	Aviation English Language Proficiency
AFM	Airplane Flight Manual
AFS	Flight Standards Service
AGL	Above Ground Level
AIM	Aeronautical Information Manual
AKTR	Airman Knowledge Test Report
ALD	Available Landing Distance
AMEL	Airplane Multiengine Land
AMES	Airplane Multiengine Sea
AOA	Angle of Attack
AOO	Area of Operation
ASEL	Airplane Single Engine Land
ASES	Airplane Single Engine Sea
ASI	Aviation Safety Inspector
ATC	Air Traffic Control
ATD	Aviation Training Device
ATP	Airline Transport Pilot
BATD	Basic Aviation Training Device
CDI	Course Deviation Indicator
CFIT	Controlled Flight Into Terrain
CFR	Code of Federal Regulations
CG	Center of Gravity
CP	Completion Phase
CRM	Crew Resource Management
CTP	Certification Training Program
DA	Decision Altitude
DH	Decision Height
DME	Distance Measuring Equipment
DP	Departure Procedures
DPE	Designated Pilot Examiner

Abb./Acronym	Definition
ELT	Emergency Locator Transmitter
FAA	Federal Aviation Administration
FADEC	Full Authority Digital Engine Control
FFS	Full Flight Simulator
FMS	Flight Management System
FSB	Flight Standardization Board
FSDO	Flight Standards District Office
FSTD	Flight Simulation Training Device
FTD	Flight Training Device
GBAS	Ground Based Augmentation System
GBAS GLS	Ground Based Augmentation Landing System
GNSS	Global Navigation Satellite System
GPS	Global Positioning System
HAT	Height Above Threshold (Touchdown)
HSI	Horizontal Situation Indicator
IA	Inspection Authorization
IAP	Instrument Approach Procedure
IFO	International Field Office
IFR	Instrument Flight Rules
IFU	International Field Unit
ILS	Instrument Landing System
IMC	Instrument Meteorological Conditions
IPC	Instrument Rating – Airplane *Canadian Conversion*
IPC	Instrument Proficiency Check
IR	Instrument Rating
IRA	Instrument Rating – Airplane
KOEL	Kinds of Operation Equipment List
LAHSO	Land and Hold Short Operations
LDA	Localizer-Type Directional Aid
LOA	Letter of Authorization
LOC	ILS Localizer
LPV	Localizer Performance with Vertical Guidance
MAP	Missed Approach Point
MDA	Minimum Descent Altitude
MEL	Minimum Equipment List
MFD	Multi-functional Displays
NAS	National Airspace System
NOD	Notice of Disapproval
NOTAMs	Notices to Airmen
NSP	National Simulator Program
NTSB	National Transportation Safety Board
PA	Private Airplane

Abb./Acronym	Definition
PAR	Private Pilot Airplane
PAT	Private Pilot Airplane/Recreational Pilot – Transition
PCP	Private Pilot Canadian Conversion
PFD	Primary Flight Display
PIC	Pilot-in-Command
POA	Plan of Action
POH	Pilot's Operating Handbook
PTS	Practical Test Standards
QPS	Qualification Performance Standard
RAIM	Receiver Autonomous Integrity Monitoring
RMP	Risk Management Process
RNAV	Area Navigation
RNP	Required Navigation Performance
SAE	Specialty Aircraft Examiner
SFRA	Special Flight Rules Area
SIAP	Standard Instrument Approach Procedure
SMS	Safety Management System
SOP	Standard Operating Procedures
SRM	Single-Pilot Resource Management
SRM	Safety Risk Management
STAR	Standard Terminal Arrival
SUA	Special Use Airspace
TAEA	Track Advisory Environmental Assessment
TAF	Terminal Forecast
TAS	True Airspeed
TCH	Threshold Crossing Height
TEM	Threat and Error Management
TFR	Temporary Flight Restrictions
UTC	Coordinated Universal Time
V_A	Maneuvering speed
VDP	Visual Descent Point
V_{FE}	Maximum flap extended speed
VFR	Visual Flight Rules
VMC	Visual Meteorological Conditions
V_{MC}	Minimum Control Speed with the Critical Engine Inoperative
V_{NE}	Never exceed speed
VOR	Very High Frequency Omnidirectional Range
V_S	Stall Speed
V_X	Best Angle of Climb Speed
V_Y	Best Rate of Climb Speed
V_{SSE}	Safe, intentional one-engine-inoperative speed. Originally known as safe single-engine speed

Abb./Acronym	Definition
V_{XSE}	Best angle of climb speed with one engine inoperative
V_{YSE}	Best rate of climb speed with one engine inoperative
V_{SO}	Stalling Speed or the Minimum Steady Flight Speed in the Landing Configuration